Infidelity Survival Plan: The Quintessential Guide to Surviving an Affair

A Proven 7 Step Plan for Healing from Infidelity and Ensuring You Avoid It in the Future

Dr. Kat Peoples

Infidelity Survival Plan: The Quintessential Guide to Surviving an Affair

A Proven 7 Step Plan for Healing from Infidelity and Ensuring You Avoid It in the Future

First Printing 2015

Copyright © 2015 - Katarzyna Peoples, Ph.D.

All Rights Reserved

Infidelity Survival Plan
Boston, MA
www.infidelitysurvivalplan.com

ISBN: 9781506126791

To all hurting couples everywhere who have even a little bit of hope that things can get better.

Table of Contents

Section 1: Why Bother?

Chapter 1:
You Are Not Alone..11

Chapter 2:
Why You Should Pause Before You React..........15

Chapter 3:
What You Don't Know....................................21

Chapter 4:
What You Can Expect....................................29

Section 2: The 7 Step Plan

Chapter 5:
A Brief Overview...47

Chapter 6:
Preparation Steps..51
    Mental Preparation.............................51
    Materials You Will Need....................54
    Emotional Preparation........................55

Chapter 7:
The 7 Step Plan...57
    Step 1:
    Right After Revealing the Betrayal...........58

Step 2:
Discuss the Affair..........................…..66
Step 3:
Reassurance & Guiding the Way…..….....68
Step 4:
Identify Reasons for the Affair…….....…...76
Step 5:
Managing Flashbacks and Obsessions…....81
Step 6:
Forgiveness……………………..…......90
Step 7:
Keeping Positive Changes Going …….…..95

Chapter 8:
What You Can Expect After Completing
the 7 Step Plan...113

Section 3: Addressing Unique Situations & Common Problems

Chapter 9:
Advanced Strategies………………....…..…..119
   When Your Partner
   Won't End the Affair……………….....119
   When Your Partner is Resistant ………...123
   A Sexually Addicted Partner……..….....124
   How to Handle Holidays
   And Special Events……………….....126
   How to Handle Relapses and Setbacks…127
   Self-Care……………………………....128
   Reintroducing Physical Intimacy………...129
   When Medication is Considered………...130

Chapter 10:
Avoiding Infidelity in the Future......................131

Chapter 11:
Preventing Sabotage...................….......…..........135
    This is Manipulative............….……....135
    Emotional Ambushes..........….............136
    Shoulds..…....137
    Comparing Your Relationship.....…......138

Chapter 12:
Conclusion...............….............................……...141

References..................................…...................145

Section 1: Why Bother?

Chapter 1: You Are Not Alone

"We cannot solve our problems with the same level of thinking that created them."

- Albert Einstein.

Debbie was pretty sure that her marriage was over. She had been married for 12 years, and she felt like she had tried everything to make things better, but things just kept getting worse with Jim. She felt like all the good times were gone forever, and they were strangers in the house. Debbie needed answers, but she felt like she had nowhere to turn.

She and Jim had gone through a lot together, but when he lost his job, and they had to rely on Debbie for income, everything seemed to get worse and worse. In the beginning, Debbie would plead with Jim to talk to her about what was wrong with him, but Jim seemed disinterested and angry. After a while, Debbie stopped trying, and they grew apart. She felt lonely and alienated from her marriage. She couldn't believe that she had arrived at this place. A few years after growing apart, Debbie discovered that Jim had been having an affair with a woman at his gym. She was angry and hurt because she felt like he had stopped working on their marriage and put his energy towards being with somebody else. When she confronted him, he denied it initially, but he finally came clean. After the admission, things just got worse. Debbie found herself being angry all the time and blaming Jim for her feelings and their unhappy marriage.

With each new accusation, Jim and Debbie grew further and further apart. Although Jim had initially stated that he wanted to work on their marriage, he continued to see the other woman.

At this point, Debbie felt like her only option was divorce. If she stayed married, she felt like she would be miserable for the rest of her life. Although they had children, she felt it was an unbearable situation for her. Debbie was torn between staying in a marriage that felt like a sham but keeping her family together and leaving with the possibility of finding happiness with another partner.

Debbie's story is similar to most of the people that I have worked with, and it may seem similar to your situation if you are reading this book. 25% of wives and 44% of husbands have had extra marital intercourse. In couples that are married or living together, straight and gay, 50% will break their vows of sexual and emotional monogamy during that relationship. While 90% of married people believe that monogamy is a priority, 50% of them admit that they have had affairs! While the statistics may seem depressing, take hope. Your marriage didn't fail because there is something wrong with you or because you and your partner were not meant to be. You just didn't have the formula. Most people don't. Being in love all by itself won't protect you from temptation. It's no wonder that infidelity is so common among loving couples.

If you are reading this book, it's safe to assume that infidelity has wrecked your relationship. You may feel like there is no hope in your marriage. You may feel like you are at the end of the line. Your partner may be unwilling to work with you on your commitment to one another. You may be torn between keeping the family together and trying to find happiness somewhere else.

These are all common thoughts and feelings. You might even have participated in couples therapy or individual therapy to work on your marriage without any success. I want you to know that there is a solution.

Most marriages that feel like they are doomed can be repaired! Most problems are solvable. I have worked with hundreds of couples struggling with their marriages and the betrayals of infidelity. While the road is no easy one, it is possible to save your marriage and make it even stronger than it ever was. Just take note: it's not about getting your marriage back anymore. It's about creating a new marriage, a stronger marriage, a happy marriage, a marriage that works, a true partnership!

You may have tried to make your feelings understood to your marriage partner and have felt like you have been chasing your partner around trying to get things to a better place with no avail. This is because talking about feelings is just part of the picture in creating successful relationships. Making feelings known does not solve the problem. Despite traditional psychotherapeutic beliefs, processing feelings is not the answer, at least not the entire answer. Bringing a feeling to the surface only brings about clarity, not solutions. There is a better way. There is a simpler way. There is a less frustrating way.

The couples that I see usually have positive results after the first session. Often, they no longer need to be seen after 10 sessions. Recovering from infidelity is a difficult process, but it is entirely possible and solvable. In this book, you will find out how to get your marriage to an even better place and heal from the betrayal.

At the end of this book, you will be in a much better place if you put these strategies into practice. You will be able to succeed because you will have the formula. That's what you need, and it's all in here.

I also talk about marriage in this program to when talking about a relationship, but if you are in a long-term monogamous relationship (no matter what the legal status), cohabitating, straight, bisexual, or gay, this book applies to you. You don't have to be married to apply these techniques so if you meet the following standards in the sentence above, keep reading. This is your formula too.

Chapter 2: Why You Should Pause Before You React

While most people in marriages feel like their relationships will succeed, today 50% of marriages end in divorce. Even more traumatic than that is the fact that infidelity is a common issue in those marriages. Couples grow apart, and a partner finds and outside lover to fill in the missing pieces of emotional and sexual intimacy. A new partner provides excitement and closeness to a spouse who has felt emotionally alienated within his or her marriage. The facts are alarming, but it makes sense when you consider that most people don't know how to be married or stay in a long-term relationship successfully.

People seek partners outside of their marriages because they feel something is missing within their relationships. While there are some unique reasons for people to cheat – like sexual addiction, for example – most cheating partners follow a familiar and predictable pattern. That pattern usually consists of filling in deficits that they feel are present in their current relationships. As I stated, in this book, you will learn how to fill in those gaps, but first, we will address how to heal from the infidelity. Healing from infidelity is most important process you must go through before you can begin making your marriage even stronger.

You may be contemplating divorce at this point. I understand that your world feels like it is falling apart, and your stomach is in knots from the extreme pain your partner has put you through.

You may feel like there is no hope, and you may feel like you don't want to do the work, but I want you to think before you decide anything about your relationship. I want you to just pause for three months. Before deciding to stay or leave, give yourself an opportunity to get some clarity about your situation and how you feel about your partner. This book will be an essential guide in your decision-making process, and by the end, you will have a good handle on what you should do.

Why Not Find a Better Partner?

Maybe you are asking yourself, "Why should I stay? My partner broke our vows so I should just leave and find someone who will treat me better. This is understandable. However, let me tell you that you are not safe from infidelity just by finding somebody else. It can happen to you again – no matter how strongly you feel connected at first. Remember the statistics. Besides, if divorce was really a good answer, people would have more successful marriages their second time around, but this just isn't true at all. Consider that the second marriage has a higher divorce rate than the first! While first marriages end in divorce 50% of the time, second marriages end in divorce 60% of the time. Often, in second marriages, divorce is due to partners not being ready for the baggage that is brought in from the first marriage. Then there's also the complexity of blended families and, of course, frustrations of previous marriages that may come into play in second marriages. Marriages take work, and finding the perfect partner is not the answer.

Another thing to consider is your children, if applicable. As long as you have children, your spouse will be an eternal part of your life.

Your spouse will always be your children's parent, and you will inevitably have to have your partner in your life anyway, whether that's physically with visitations or emotionally with feedback from children or perhaps complaints about an absent parent. Children, of course, are also negatively affected by divorce. Children take divorce very hard, and whether they are young or grown, divorce makes a severe impact on a child. Of course, there are some instances where you may need to leave the marriage (if you are being physically abused, for example), but in most cases, a marriage can be improved even when infidelity has occurred. In fact, infidelity challenges and getting through those challenges have often strengthened marriages! You just have to know how to do that.

You may be wondering, if we were meant to be together, my partner would never have cheated on me. This just simply isn't true. People are attracted to other people naturally. We wouldn't be human if we weren't attracted to people around us. Marriage does not dissolve this fact. Just because your partner has chosen to step outside of your marriage, does not mean that you are with the wrong person. If you and your partner had a loving relationship in the beginning and you both enjoyed each other and felt like you were meant to be together, you can get this back. Actually, you can be stronger than you ever were.

There may be a reason you know about the affair. How did you find out? Did you see your partner's email? Did a text come through that wasn't meant for you? Did you get suspicious because things just didn't seem right between you?

Were there suspicious actions? In many cases, something will tip you off. This is actually a positive sign for you relationship. Research has shown that carelessness of a partner who has cheated might signal a desire to be caught.

Isn't that something? That there were signs of the infidelity signals your partner's subconscious desire to end the madness of the double life. Here's another reassuring statistic – only 10% of affairs end in marriage. This means that the affair partner usually isn't the right person for your partner anyway.

I want you also to know that your partner does not have to be involved in the healing process at first. If your partner is not willing to work on your marriage, you can start the journey of healing on your own. Eventually, your partner will need to cooperate in the process if he or she is unwilling now, but for now, you can just worry about yourself. Just know that the partner that has cheated has to be the healer in the end. If your partner is not willing to work on your marriage, skip to chapter 9 of this book and go to "When Your Partner is Resistant." I give you strategies there to start the process on your own. After your partner has committed, you can begin the 7 Step healing process in Chapter 7.

Let me tell you that you will see results after a few steps of working the plan. Minor changes will make big differences. While no marriage is exactly the same, and no one strategy will solve all marital problems across the board, rest assured that there are multiple strategies that work. In Chapter 7, I provide you with the step-by-step 7 Step Plan for healing from the infidelity and transforming your marriage to a strong and happy partnership that you always wanted.

If you follow the steps in the plan, your marriage will improve and you will get through this better than you ever thought. In some instances, you may decide that you need to leave the marriage.

After reading this book and apply the interventions, you will know you have made the right decision, whether you choose to leave or stay in your marriage. However, I find that most spouses end up working things out and working through the betrayal quite successfully.

After reading through the program, you will have the tools to work through the intense betrayal of infidelity, and you will also have the tools to create a stronger marriage. Do not blame yourself. The infidelity was not your fault. In fact, blame is unproductive in this journey. While it is tempting to blame your partner for being a cheater and an awful spouse, the blame game is unproductive so throw it aside. However, I realize that you will need to work through obsessive thoughts and hurtful feelings. You may not be there right now, but eventually you will look at your spouse as the healer. This is what your partner will become. In most cases, if both of you work through the steps together, your marriage will be sensational. You might even be thankful that the infidelity became a part of your life because, without it, you wouldn't have ever gained what you did by going through this program. Now that's something to look forward to!

Chapter 3: What You Don't Know

Couples are misguided when they suffer from such a huge betrayal and try to get back to the place where they were when they first fell in love. You may be thinking to yourself, "I want us to get back to where we were before." Take that out of your mind – looking back is unproductive here. In fact, getting what you had back is impossible. However, this is a good thing. While it might seem like a wonderful idea, the goal of getting back to where you were in the first place is a request for additional failure. You're here for a reason. Your marriage probably wasn't as strong as you thought it was. This is not to say, in any way, that the affair is your fault. However, infidelity happened because there were problems in the marriage, whether that was growing apart due to busy lives or fighting over money. Small things can create huge problems over time, as you probably know.

You can infidelity-proof your marriage by following the program that I set up for you in this book. But first, let's review some misconceptions that couples have about monogamy and what a good marriage is. There are many reasons marriages go bad, and then couples wonder, what happened? We were so in love, and now our marriage is totally torn apart. How did we get here? Let me answer those questions for you first.

The Stages of a Marriage

All marriages go through three stages, but most people don't notice the transitions or think that something has gone wrong when they enter into a more difficult yet natural progression.

Stage 1: Honeymoon

Everyone knows about the honeymoon stage, right? This is when the two individuals of a couple are enamored with one another and nothing seems to be wrong with the other. What happens after that? Of course, as you know, the honeymoon stage fades away, and another stage begins, a more difficult stage.

Stage 2: The Storm

This second stage is the stormy stage. In the stormy stage, the couple starts seeing faults in the other. Expectations about the way something "should be" or what a partner "should be doing" get in the way of reality as both individuals in the relationship are in the process of learning how to be with the other while managing personal expectations learned from past family roles. Disagreements are common, and butting heads is a part of the storming process. Unfortunately, many couples never transition out of this stage. They continue to butt heads and argue, blaming the other for being wrong for one reason or another. All couples need to pass through this stage to get to a healthy long-term intimate relationship.

While the stormy stage is very normal, many couples think that there is something wrong with their relationship when they enter the stage because, all of a sudden, they are no longer getting along. Because of this, some couples determine that they are in a bad marriage or that they married the wrong person.

Arguments continue, and distance prevails. Other couples weather the storm and are able to transition to the third stage, the collaborative stage. This is the stage where both partners are working together well and the relationship is stable.

Stage 3: Collaboration

Couples who weather the storm of the second stage usually come out with a greater commitment to one another and a stronger bond than they had before. They reach collaboration, and they know how to work through difficulties together. In this stage, they are team members in life, love, and everything else.

These three stages are a broad overview of the experiences that most marriages go through as they negotiate their relationship. It is probably safe to say that you are still in the stormy stage, and I'm not sure if you ever left there in the first place. You might have gotten to the collaborative stage and stressors might have brought you and your partner back into a stormy place. Either way, you are reading this book because your marriage is not in a place where you want it to be, and you are looking for guidance. In this program, if you choose to work on your relationship with your partner, you can get to the third stage - collaboration. However, for now, we need to focus on helping you heal from the betrayal of infidelity.

The Monogamy Myth

Before discussing the program any further, let me tell you a little secret about monogamy. You may find it surprising, but monogamy is not a natural condition for human beings, and because of this, it is not easy to maintain.

Monogamy takes a lot of work and commitment. We are constantly straying with our eyes and with our emotions. We are always capable of being attracted to others outside of our marriage. This is a fact. I think a lot of people get into trouble that way.

Don't think for a minute that "we are meant to be. I will never look at anybody else in the same way that I look at my spouse." This just isn't true. You will be attracted to someone outside of your marriage, and so will your spouse. The trick is to protect your marriage in a way that these attractions do not turn into threats or infidelities.

In their book, *The Myth of Monogamy: Fidelity and Infidelity in Animals and People*, Barash and Lipton inform us that monogamy does not come naturally. In fact, they state that biologists have discovered that members of many species cheat. Cheating is the rule rather than the exception among all sexes! Humans are part of this equation. This may seem depressing to you, but it is actually liberating. Monogamy takes work. It does not come naturally, and it doesn't just happen on its own. Just because you are with somebody whom you love and who loves you does not mean that infidelity is not a potential hazard. I think the myth of monogamy is exceptionally dangerous because people think that their marriages should just work because love alone should conquer all. It doesn't. Relationships take work. While we hear this all the time, I don't think that most people believe that. I don't think that most people know how to work on their relationships.

This is not only a guide for getting through infidelity, but it is also a manual to strengthen your marriage. The fact is that monogamy works very well for most people. One of our unique traits about being human is our ability to overcome our biology. Isn't that something?

Just because we are naturally inclined to not be monogamous does not mean that it isn't what is best for us. Most people are monogamous for a reason. Monogamy works very well for most people. Just because it's not natural doesn't mean that it's not the best decision for you.

I think the concept of knowing that monogamy is not natural is just an avenue to strengthen your marriage because you really realize that you have to work on your marriage. You have to do the work. You have to put in the effort in order to overcome your biology. If you know this from the beginning, you are prepared for the work that is ahead instead of assuming that your marriage will just naturally be monogamous. Monogamy is a rarity in the animal species. We humans choose it because we feel it is the best choice for us.

Even if you decided that you cannot stay in your current relationship because the infidelity is too much for you to deal with, you will need a lot of this knowledge from this book in order to work towards your next relationship. You want a strong marriage, and, in most instances, you can't have that without the formula. Don't assume that your marriage will be blissful and infidelity-free if you move on to another partner. This is dangerous thinking. With all that said, I want to urge you to take some time before deciding whether you want to leave your marriage or if you want to stay to work things out.

As you give yourself three months to think it through, don't think of this time as staying in your marriage. Think about it as a time of reflection. If you have just discovered your partner's infidelity, things will change day to day and week to week. You will feel like staying one day and throwing in the towel the next. You will experience a bunch of emotional peaks and valleys, and this is why the first three months after discovery is not a good time to make any decision about your relationship.

The program you will be reading about is framed around 7 Steps, and when you get finished reading this book, you will have a much better idea of what to do. Give yourself the three-month waiting time to decide.

You probably have a lot of difficult questions that might keep coming up for you: Will I ever be able to forget? How can I ever learn to trust again? What should I tell the children? How can I handle the pain that I feel? Will my marriage ever be good again? Should I stay or should I throw in the towel?

While it may be hard to believe, your marriage can be even better than you thought after the affair, but you must do the work. If you learn how to handle all the terrible days ahead and the traumatic reactions that you might have, a strong and happy marriage is possible. It will be a difficult road ahead on many levels, but you can do this. I have helped hundreds of couples who have been betrayed, and I have constructed this program so that you can do it on your own. In the program, I focus on helping you get through the pain, manage negative feelings, and repair your marriage through solution-oriented methods rather than years and years of painful trauma work. While it will take time, it will not take years for you to get to a better place.

Having a difficult time is normal after the discovery of an affair but remember that the first few months are not the best time to make clearheaded decisions because you are so emotionally wrought with pain and confusion. You are not able to judge the viability of your partnership when you are feeling hurt and, in some cases, revengeful. Give yourself the space to think before you act.

You may be tempted to walk out the door because you think that the pain will go away if you leave, but I assure you that the pain will still be there. You will need to get through the betrayal on your own or with your spouse.

Either way, you will need to heal, and it will not be an easy process, no matter which direction you decide to go in your marriage. If you go through the pain with your spouse, you can get out on the other side with an even better marriage then you have ever thought possible.

But We Already Tried Therapy

If you have been to therapy before, you might be suspicious about getting expert help because it may not have worked for you in the past. Many couples that I have worked with have said to me, "We talked a bunch about how we felt, but my therapist never gave me any ways to change our situation. I was really frustrated, and we just ended up fighting more."

While feelings are a big part of the process, they are not the entire process if change is to come and be effective. When my clients leave my office, they have a plan to work in between sessions.

It is not too late to save your marriage. If you even have the slightest interest in working things out with your spouse, I can show you how. At this point, however, all you need to do is read on. Whether you decide to leave or stay, you will use the tools that I provide for you in your future relationship if you want it to be successful.

Chapter 4:
What You Can Expect

An affair is extremely traumatic. It is also dangerous and potentially lethal to the relationship. However, when a couple takes the steps of healing and works on the steps, as outlined in this program, the affair actually provides new insights and even better interactions within the marriage. In fact, relationships are often better than they were before. It might be impossible to even imagine it, but many couples have been thankful to have gone through the healing process of an affair. Granted, they never would want to walk through it again, but looking back, they realize how much stronger their marriage is and realize that they couldn't have gotten to this place without the initial trauma. If you follow the steps of this program, you, most likely, will have the same experience.

Imagine having a strong marriage, one where you are in love with your spouse again and your spouse is in love with you. You confide in one another. You trust one another. You are stable in your relationship and know that your partner will always put you first, and you do the same for your partner. As you look back on the affair, you can't believe how far you've come and as crazy as it may seem, you are grateful to have gone through the process. You are no longer roommates sharing a house and raising children together. The distance you once felt between the two of you is gone and the fights are no longer toxic and destructive. When you and your partner have an argument, you solve problems together.

You and your partner put each other first and you discuss your relationship and how it is going between the two of you on a regular basis. Imagine that you feel informed and fully safe in your marriage for the very first time in years. You no longer having to feel those feelings of betrayal and no longer obsessing about where your spouse is going day to day. Flashbacks are no longer an issue, and when you watch a program on television that used to trigger feelings of betrayal, those toxic feelings you used to feel seem like a distant memory. Your friends and family cannot believe how far you and your spouse have come, and though they had their doubts about your spouse when both of you were in the thick of it, they are impressed with how the two of you are treating one another now. How things have changed.

Friends who you thought had better marriages then yours (of course, that might have been almost all your friends back then!) now come to you for advice when they are struggling. "How did you and your spouse get through it?" they ask you. "The two of you are like two peas in a pod now, and I can't believe you are the same couple." But you aren't the same couple anymore, are you? No.

You and your spouse, after completing this program, have reached a different level in your marriage and you are both different people because of it. You and your partner know how to communicate. When there is something that is bothering you, you know how to bring it up to your spouse, and your spouse listens to your concerns. What a difference!

When your spouse has to go out of town for business, you no longer worry that there will be a betrayal. You know that the trust is strong and that you are both in a good place.

You talk regularly to one another when you are not together, and when you are together, you genuinely enjoy each other's company. You are a shining example for the friends and family in your life and you can barely believe how good your marriage is.

Though it was tough, you are in a better place than you ever thought you could be. This is where this program can take you if you follow the steps. Most couples see success and are able to heal from the infidelity very well. Their marriages are stronger than ever, and they have rebuilt trust in their relationships. Although some people do decide to move on because they feel that their marriages cannot be saved, most people build a better partnership. In most cases, it is not about the person you are with but about the work that you are willing to do. You both need to do the work, and though it will be difficult at times, this program will help you see small glimmers of hope along the way.

No marriage is perfect. Every relationship is a work in progress, and I do not want you to think that your relationship will be perfect at the end of this program. However, it will be in a much better place, and you will have the tools to continue to work on your marriage and make it better and better year after year. This program is not just about healing from infidelity. It's much more than that. It is also about making your marriage infidelity-proof. To do that, your marriage needs to be strong in order to accomplish it, and I have constructed a program for you to be able to get to that place.

If you and your partner are willing to do the work, you will be amazed at the results. But don't worry. It only takes one to get positive changes started in a relationship. If your partner is not willing to do any of the work yet, things might still turn around for you. In the end, alone or together, you will be whole again.

In the next few pages, you can read about success stories of individuals who have gone through this program and the results they had. While the details are true, I have changed names and demographic information to protect the anonymity of the individuals I have helped.

All the details within the success stories are true, and I have provided them here to show you the range of progress that can be made if you follow the program I have outlined in this book. I highlighted only the cases where clients have contacted me a few years after therapy. This is done purposefully because I want you to see long-term results are possible with this program. If they can do it, so can you!

Donna and Andrew

Donna came into my office a few days after she had discovered that her husband, Andrew, had been having an affair with his coworker Janice. She was completely distraught and she didn't know whether she wanted to work on her marriage or leave, but she knew that she could not stand feeling what she was feeling. She felt so betrayed and so hurt by what Andrew had done. After nine years of marriage and two children, she never saw it coming. Donna told me that she and Andrew had grown apart after the birth of their second child. Because her second child had special needs, Donna was spending a lot more time trying to help her son and had less time for Andrew. Although she realized that the distance between the two of them had been there, she never thought that Andrew would cheat on her with another woman. She discovered the affair by logging into his email account one day and finding an email from Janice.

It was sexual in nature, and when Donna read it, her stomach dropped and she couldn't believe what she was reading. She confronted Andrew that night and he denied it initially, but when she told him that she read the email, Andrew admitted to the affair.

He said that he still wanted to work things out with Donna, and he didn't know what he was thinking. Donna was so angry and so hurt that she didn't know how to handle the situation. She immediately made an appointment for therapy, and this is how she ended up at my office.

First and foremost, I told Donna to give herself 12 weeks before she made a decision about her marriage. Because her emotions were all over the place, Donna was not in a position to make a decision about saving her marriage or leaving. I told her to put that on hold while we worked together. Since Andrew was willing to work on their marriage, Donna brought him in for a few sessions in the beginning, and this was a very positive thing. After a month, Andrew and Donna decided that they wanted to work on their marriage because it was worth saving. They also had children to consider, and Donna did not want to break the family apart. Although she was still very angry with Andrew for having an affair, she was able to get some clarity and felt like working on the marriage was a good decision, at least for practical reasons, at that point.

I worked with Andrew and Donna for about three months, and the progress was very quick. Because both partners will willing to work on the marriage and go through the program that I prescribed, positive changes began happening within the first few sessions. It took some time for Donna to begin trusting Andrew again, but that progressed eventually.

After three months, Andrew and Donna were pretty well on their way to a great marriage. I saw Andrew and Donna every few weeks just for "maintenance" requests. Donna still felt like she had some work to do in the trust department, but mostly, she enjoyed going to couples therapy with Andrew.

They went from distant partners dealing with infidelity to being in love again like they were when they first met. Their marriage was much more mature, however, and they were able to tackle problems in their relationship like they never could before. This was particularly helpful with the responsibilities they had with their son who had special needs.

Donna felt that Andrew supported her like he had never supported her before, and they became true partners in the parenting department, as well as lovers and best friends. I still get an email from Donna from time to time after several years, and she tells me that she and Andrew are still doing better than ever. The "maintenance" tools that I provided for them had been life savers when they arrived at a place where they felt stuck.

In this book, you will also learn the same maintenance tools I provided for Donna and Andrew so that you also can keep your positive changes going in your marriage. Your relationship will take work year after year, even when the healing has finished, and you and your partner will be truly better for it.

Jillian and Allison

Jillian loved Allison, but she just couldn't bring herself to get past the betrayal. After five years of being together, Allison stepped out of the relationship into the arms of another woman.

Jillian came to me after finding out about the affair, and she was very sure that she no longer wanted to work on the relationship. After three months of thinking about it and discussing options in therapy, Jillian decided that she still felt she needed to move on from the relationship.

She wanted badly to start a family, and she felt as if Allison would not be able to meet that need as both of them were approaching their 40s. Jillian did not feel that she would be able to heal enough to feel stable in the relationship to start a family. After meeting with both of them for a couples session, Allison and Jillian both decided that it would be a better idea to move on from the relationship.

Despite my opinion that they could work through their issues, neither partner was willing to do the work so I continued to work with Jillian to help her through the healing process on her own. Jillian struggled with obsessiveness and insecurity because of Allison's betrayal. She felt like she could never trust another partner again, and she was terrified that she would make huge mistakes in a future relationship. Because of these fears, Jillian was paralyzed and could not move forward into another relationship. We worked together for five months, and I taught her how to manage flashbacks and obsessive thoughts when they came about. We also worked on how to create a relationship that is open and honest.

While infidelity is very common, it is a preventable thing, in most cases. While there are exceptions, such as sexual addiction issues, most couples suffer through infidelity because the relationship is not well. Aggravation creates distance, and distance creates loneliness. After some time, one partner will confide in somebody else, and as boundaries get blurred with outsiders, infidelity can be the result.

After working together, Jillian was able to understand how a relationship works and how she could control her part of a relationship so that she could see the signs of infidelity. Better yet, we worked on how to create a relationship where infidelity is not an issue.

Because Jillian understood how infidelity happened and what she could do to prevent infidelity in her next relationship, she was able to trust again. After a year, I heard from Jillian who said that she started a new relationship with a woman she met in her church group. She felt hopeful and optimistic about the relationship, and she felt that she was armed with enough information to be able to make this relationship a success.

Four years later, Jillian sent me an email letting me know that she and her partner were still together and using many of the tools that I taught her in therapy years ago. They were planning a wedding that year, and she emailed me to thank me for giving her hope again and allowing her to find trust in another partner. Of course, Jillian did all the work; I just gave her the tools. She was an extremely motivated client, and she followed my program to the letter. It was so rewarding to see that even years after leaving therapy, she was still using the tools that I taught her to use, and they were still working.

These tools are all provided in this book for you. Whether you are working on moving on from your current relationship or, as I hope, you stay in your current relationship and work on repairing it with your partner, this book will be vital for your success. I taught Janice that long-term relationships have a formula, and as long as she remembers the formula and uses the tools, she will succeed, in most cases. And she did.

Evelyn and Martin

Evelyn began therapy with me after Martin moved out of the house. She had discovered he had been having an affair for months before arriving in my office. They tried to work it out in the beginning.

Martin had recently decided that their marriage would never be good again so he moved out to be with his mistress. Evelyn was devastated, and she had three children with Martin, two who were under the age of five. She was overwhelmed, and she didn't know where to turn. She wanted to work on her marriage, and she was devastated Martin had given up on them.

Martin never stopped talking to his mistress when she and Martin finally decided that they would try to work on their marriage, and Evelyn found herself at an ultimate low. Not only had he deserted his children, he had deserted 17 years of marriage to be with a woman he only met a year ago. When Evelyn came into my office, she was in tears and didn't think that there was any hope for her marriage. While she wanted to work things out with Martin, he had completely pulled away from her, and she was left alone in the house with three children and no support.

I told Evelyn that she could begin making changes on her own, and while the tactics that I taught her would not guarantee that Martin would come back, she had a much better shot of him returning if she changed some of her behaviors. Martin still came around every few days for the children so they had interactions weekly. I told Evelyn of how she could change the way that she approached Martin, and she was an apt pupil. Evelyn and I discussed a plan, and she set it into motion the following day when Martin came to pick up the children.

In our next session, two weeks later, Evelyn came to my office overjoyed. While Martin was still not moved back into the home, he had changed his attitude towards her significantly. He was much nicer to her again and interested in what she was doing. He was also talking about reconciliation.

Evelyn and I worked for another three weeks together before Martin came into session to start couples counseling with Evelyn. Because of the changes Evelyn made and how she approached Martin, Martin changed the way he felt about her and his marriage.

They were both hopeful again that they could come to a place where their marriage was good again. I worked with Evelyn and Martin four months after to help Evelyn heal from the betrayal and to help them both build trust and emotional intimacy. It has been seven years now, and Evelyn and Martin are better than ever. I still see Evelyn and Martin from time to time for "maintenance" sessions, once or twice a year. They like to check in and assess where they are in their marriage and what they can work on further.

While most of the couples that I see don't continue years after with me for any maintenance, Evelyn and Martin wanted to incorporate this in their couples work, and I was glad to help them in this venture. It was wonderful me to see how their marriage had progressed and how much better they are doing year after year.

Evelyn started therapy with a broken marriage, and now she has a strong relationship with the man she fell in love with, and they are raising all three of their children together as a team. "I never thought we would get here," Evelyn said in session one day. "I was completely hopeless, and going to therapy on my own was just something that I needed to do, but I never dreamed that this would actually work."

Well, it did, and Evelyn and Martin are still doing well today. It only takes one person to get the process of change started, and if you are on your own in this marriage and your spouse has left you, you will learn some tactics of how to be able to save your marriage despite starting alone.

While it is not a guarantee your spouse will come back, I have found that, in many cases, this is just what happens. It just takes some changes in the right direction.

Most Problems Can Be Solved

Did you know that it is a common belief among many therapists that most marriages and relationships will end with breaking up even after couples therapy? It is not uncommon for many clinicians to think that couples therapy is just the beginning of the end because as many say, "One partner always has a foot out the door anyway."

I am here to tell you that this is a common belief because many therapists do not know how to successfully work with troubled married couples. I know because I was one of them too! Let me explain.

Most therapists discuss feelings and childhood traumas with their married couples because they understand that the realizations couples make about why they do what they do solves problems. As I said, I held this belief too, but throughout the years, I have found this to be untrue. When I used to counsel couples towards the beginning of my career, I would grow increasingly frustrated over the lack of progress that I saw. I would feel stuck just as the couple would feel stuck.

Often, I would hear, "I know that I act this way because of the way I grew up and the relationship I have with my father, but how do I stop doing it?" Time after time, I would feel stuck because the knowledge did not solve anything. I knew that there had to be a better way.

Because I was trained traditionally in Psychology, I understood human suffering in a particular way, and I thought that discussing feelings and traumas was the primary way to go.

What I have found throughout my years of working with couples is that discussing feelings and past experiences is only part of the picture. In fact, sometimes people do not need to revisit childhood traumas in order to improve their marriages. While the information is helpful and brings about clarity, I found that it does not often bring about change. People understanding why they do what they do does not stop them from doing those things. Despite the guidance of Freud, trudging through childhood trauma in order for that knowledge to heal all wounds is ineffective, and I have not found this to be effective when working with couples.

I realized that I needed a new way to help the couples in my practice, and I put my ego aside and tried to find the answer for the people that I worked with. I could no longer think that most of the married couples I worked with were resistant to change or that they really didn't want it badly enough. It had to be me that was failing, not them.

I also gave up on the concept that both partners needed to commit to counseling before any positive changes could occur. This just simply isn't true. However, many therapists believe this and are unable to help a struggling individual trying badly to get the marriage back on track despite having to work at it alone.

Lastly, I believe that couples who are on the brink of separation or divorce need some immediate evidence or at least some hope that things can get better. Psychoanalytic theory did not provide me with that avenue, and many couples ended up frustrated with one another from the beginning of therapy, making the problem even worse.

As I started to research marital therapy further, I found that most professionals didn't agree on how to effectively work with couples. Gestalt therapists worked on completing processes and staying in the here and now.

Psychoanalysts focused on childhood traumas and on bringing unconscious thoughts into the conscious mind. Adlerian therapists focused on birth order and so on and so on. This was really frustrating for me because I wanted to find the formula that worked for couples, and what I found was a lot of ineffective theories and fruitless strategies.

After some time, I found the best formula for helping couples and started to see positive results in my practice. Couples were no longer frustrated and splitting up. They were finding hope that their problems could be solved, and they were seeing real positive changes, often after their first sessions.

With a mix of meaning-making strategies and behavioral modifications, I discovered a solution that works. I no longer wanted to be the therapist that couples talked about as ineffective – "We talked about feelings and our childhoods, but we have no idea what we're supposed to do to change our marriage." No, now, all of my couples know exactly what to do after leaving each session with me, and they go home working on a clear plan that creates immediate change.

Through the years, case after case, I have had couples report significant positive changes after just a few sessions, often after the first session, without having to dig into the past and deal with childhood traumas. This is not to say that exploring past childhood traumas and feelings is not effective because it is certainly effective for long-term growth and change. I still continue to process the past in long-term therapy for many clients, and I, by no means, am dismissing the effectiveness of psychoanalysis and other theories that subscribe to a primary-feelings model. While there is a time and a place for those explorations, it's not the best place to start.

I have found that couples on the brink of divorce are not aided effectively in the beginning by these modes of helping. Struggling couples need action, and talking on and on about problems is not initially effective.

You will have positive results quickly. Relationships are about patterns and habits that have developed over the years, and I show couples how to change those patterns so that they can make major differences in their relationships. This is done through behavioral interventions, and as a traditionally trained therapist, I had to make some changes in that area.

I was trained to understand that therapy is effective only through processing feelings and the past, but I had to put my ego aside and deny that. I had to do what worked and change my pattern, and now, so will you!

I wrote this book in an effort to help couples understand that they can heal from infidelity and that they can save their marriages, making them better than they ever thought before.

While many couples have benefited from working with me and repairing their marriages, I felt like I was barely making a dent in helping individuals realize that their marriages are worth saving. Knowing that 50% of marriages end in divorce, and that infidelity is more common than we like to admit, I felt I had to spread the word more effectively and make these practical principles and tools available to struggling couples.

Even more than that, I wanted to provide people with the information on how to infidelity-proof their marriages. Why go through the healing process from infidelity if you can avoid it in the first place? While nothing is guaranteed, this book will provide you with the best chance for success on every level.

Because of the betrayal that you suffered, you might be thinking that you want a divorce. You might be thinking that your marriage is not worth saving and that you will never heal from what happened.

Maybe it is your spouse who wants to leave or will not give up the affair partner. Maybe you think that divorce is the only way to improve your life. However, I have to believe that because you are reading this book, you have some hope that your marriage will work. Perhaps you are reading this book because you want to heal on your own.

I want to urge you again to take three months before you make any decision about your marriage. If you are, in the least bit hopeful that somehow, you and your spouse will love each other once again, keep reading. It is not too late to save your marriage, and it is not too late to heal from the wounds of infidelity. If you even have the smallest interest in working towards saving your marriage, I can promise you that the possibility of change is very realistic.

I cannot tell you how many couples I have worked with who thought that their marriage was beyond saving and came to therapy as a last resort. So many of these couples have turned things around and are stronger than ever for it. You can be that couple. You can heal from this intense pain that you feel. You can make your marriage stronger than it ever was before. You can do this.

Section 2: How to Use the 7 Step Plan

Chapter 5:
A Brief Overview

"The best relationships in our lives are the best not because they have been the happiest ones, they are that way because they have stayed strong through the most tormentful of storms."

— Pandora Poikilos,
Excuse Me, My Brains Have Stepped Out

Jennifer was devastated when she found out that Tim had an affair with another woman. They had been together for 14 years, and while they had problems in their marriage, Jennifer thought that for the most part, they were happy. The past few years had been rough due to Jennifer having to take care of her ill mother, and she and Tim spoke less and less and worked more and more. She never dreamt that Tim would betray her in this way, especially since she had been caring for her ill mother all this time and had been having such a rough emotional time dealing with her imminent death.

They came to see me for therapy a few months after Tim's affair was discovered. They had tried to work it out together, but Jennifer just grew more and more insecure about Tim's commitment to her, and Tim grew more and more distant with all of Jennifer's questions and accusations. At this point in their marriage, Tim was even more distant and angry, and he was resistant to giving up his affair partner.

Jennifer, of course, grew more insecure and angrier at Tim's behavior, but she wanted to keep their marriage together because she loved him and she knew that he loved her too. In the first session, we outlined the issue at hand and the immediate problems that needed to be addressed. We worked on solutions. Tim and Jennifer left my office with clear goals and a concrete plan to work on until we met again for our next session. After two weeks, Tim and Jennifer met me for their next appointment and things had gotten significantly better. Jennifer was no longer plaguing Tim with accusations, and Tim was more forthcoming with the details of his affair. He had also called his affair partner in front of Jennifer to break it off, letting his affair partner know that he was committed to his wife and wanted to focus on working on his marriage.

I worked with them in the second session to refine the plan a bit more and to start working on long-term behaviors that would help them mend their broken marriage. After a few months of working together as a couple and refining goals every few weeks, Jennifer and Tim felt that they were in a good place, and we finished therapy. Jennifer felt more secure about their relationship, and Tim was more forthcoming with the information she needed. He was also more supportive of her needs as the betrayed partner.

After only a year, Tim contacted me via email to let me know that their marriage was better than it had ever been before. Although he would never want to hurt Jennifer again and was regretful of the decisions he had made having an affair, he was, in a strange way, thankful that the trauma had happened. He told me that they would never be as good as they are now without having to have gone through the healing process.

You can, without a doubt, get through the betrayal of this affair and make your marriage stronger than ever, just as Jennifer and Tim did. In a matter of months, you can be in a much better place than you are right now.

In fact, after you apply just a few of these techniques, you will start to see immediate positive results. While your marriage won't be perfect, and you won't be healed completely from the betrayal, you will be well on your way to a better future after just the first few interventions. It has been my experience with the couples that I have helped that healing happens much quicker in the marriage than they anticipated. Though the road is not easy, it is doable, and I have seen hundreds of couple succeed through the application tips I outline for you in this book.

First and foremost, I focus on solutions rather than problems. To help you heal from the infidelity, you will need to feel your feelings, and there is no escape from that. However, I don't believe in focusing on the problem in such a tedious manner that solutions are overlooked. You will get solutions first, and those problems that you are tackling will be resolved. Forget about revisiting childhood traumas. I won't take you there, and it is unnecessary to take you there. While this tactic is very effective for long-term intimacy, it is not something that is needed in the beginning.

My emphasis for your healing your marriage is on observable behaviors and concrete tools to get you through the hurtful feelings. I will help you tackle obsessive thoughts, conquer flashbacks, and show you how to rebuild your marriage.

You will also learn how to keep the positive changes going in your marriage for years to come. I also provide you with a troubleshooting section for times when you feel that you and your partner are not progressing as well as you think you should be. You will never get your marriage back; you will have a new marriage, and it will be a better marriage.

Chapter 6: Preparation Steps

Even though age can bring about wisdom through experience, it can also hinder our progress because of shortsightedness and disabling assumptions. In this chapter, I want to introduce you to some vital ingredients for preparing for this program. Remember that you will be thinking in different ways and shifting assumptions that you have carried with you for years. With this said, I want to prepare you so that you will be the most successful you can be in working through this program. Think of this chapter as the tool kit for your successful journey – now on to what you will need to prepare for this program.

Mental Preparation

Motivation

If you are motivated to change, you can start the process on your own. As I said, you do not need your spouse to begin making changes in your relationship. I have helped many individuals change their relationships without their partners being present in therapy at first. You might be thinking, "Why do I always have to be the person that puts forth all of the effort?" You don't, of course, but I have to say that since you're the one reading this book, you are probably the one that will begin the process.

It's not about who was right and who was wrong, but it's about who will start making the changes in order for positive progress to begin. Someone needs to begin so it might as well be you.

You will need motivation, but you will see that by making small changes, you will see results pretty quickly in your relationship. If your partner is willing to do the work with you and wants to work on your relationship, you are in a better spot to begin and while the process will not be easy, there will be progress, and it will be observable. The motivation you will need will be to understand that small steps are part of the process to a big finish.

While you might get frustrated at times because you see your partner shifting back into old behaviors or you might do the same with your old behaviors, you will need the motivation to remind yourself that this program is about small steps and that the more that you work through problematic areas, the better your relationship will become. Motivation is needed throughout the program, but the first few months will be difficult for you if you are healing from the betrayal of infidelity so keep it in the forefront of your mind.

A Novice Mind

As we age, we obtain a lot of wisdom. As I said before, that wisdom might also get in the way. We get stuck in our shortsightedness and believe that things should be a certain way. As we age, it is more difficult to change, not because it is impossible but because we get stuck in our narrow minded thinking. For this program to work for you, you must be a novice. Let go of your expectations and the way that you think things should function and begin with a mind that is clear of judgments.

This program is here to help you improve your relationship and heal from the infidelity, and you will need to go through a series of changes in order for that to happen.

Remember that the old things that you've been doing have not worked to better your relationship so when you get to the point of reconciliation with your spouse, if that is what you choose to do, clear your mind and read as a novice. Because of the betrayal, you are probably looking at your life and your relationship through a certain lens, and that lens is probably dimmed by negative thoughts and expectations. This is understandable. However, try to set negative and pessimistic thoughts aside as you read through the chapters of this book, and open up your mind to new expectations. In order for you to heal and resolve your current relationship or make a future relationship better than it would have been, you need to be open to a new process.

Small Steps to a Big Finish

The changes that I discuss in this book will provide you with small accomplishments along the way to building a fulfilling relationship and a healed heart. However, you will be frustrated as setbacks occur so remember that little by little, you will get to your goal. It will take time, but you will get there if you diligently work through the steps.

Here's the good news. The progress that you will see, as small as some of it may seem, will be pretty immediate so it will be important for you to take note of the positive changes occurring day to day in your relationship so that you stay motivated. The way that you think and feel about your partner because of the betrayal that you have lived through will begin to change in a more positive manner.

Small steps may seem like flukes at times, and this is why the documentation of those small steps is so important. You can take comfort in knowing that there is change being made.

Some Pain is Unavoidable

In order for you to heal from the infidelity, you will need to feel your feelings and tune in to them at times. While you will learn many strategies to help you work through obsessive thoughts and flashbacks, initially, you will need to fully feel the hurt. This, by no means, will be a torturous road that you will have to walk on for years and years, as that would be too difficult for a relationship to survive. However, initially, the pain will be imminent. You cannot expect that you will omit all the negative feelings out of your life in the very beginning. This is not what healing is about, and no program will be successful without going through those feelings of pain. It will be a roller coaster, but you won't fall out if you trust the process.

Materials You Will Need

A Progress journal

You just need two materials for this program – a writing utensil and a notebook. Before you start the program, buy a new notebook and grab a pen or pencil to note the positive changes that have been occurring throughout the program. Keeping a journal will be the key tool to keep your motivation going and realize that positive changes are occurring, however small they might be. This journal is your key to keeping up your motivation and positive outlook throughout the process.

You will also learn how to use this journal to note positive changes that have been occurring (along with other notations), but for now, just understand that you will need this tool for this program to be effective.

Emotional Preparation

Emotions will ambush you from time to time so be prepared for these challenges. This is why the progress journal is so essential in this program. In those times when you feel discouraged and you wonder if anything is going well throughout this program, your journal will be the tool you need to get you through those negative and self-defeating times.

Patience

You will see a positive results quickly, but total healing and reparation will take some time and you will need patience throughout this process. At times, things may not go the way that you would want them to go or certain strategies may not work the way that you had wished they had worked. This is why I give you different strategies for different challenges, as every couple is not the same. Be open to trying a few strategies and remember that patience is a very important and indispensable element of this journey.

Chapter 7:
The 7 Step Plan

I realize that you may be reading this book thinking that you don't know if you want to reconcile with your spouse. This is understandable, and you want to give yourself that time to decide if it is worth the work. However, this plan is written in a way that assumes that you do want reconciliation. Nevertheless, if you choose to end your relationship with your partner, you still will be able to use the healing steps outlined in this program for yourself and learn how to build a strong relationship in your future. So, in any case, this book will be extremely powerful and pertinent to whatever decision you might make along the way.

Each step in this program assumes spousal cooperation, and, of course, this is not always the case as defensiveness and resistance can be an inevitable part of working things out. If you encounter resistance from your partner from one step to the next, I provide you with strategies in Chapter 9 so that you can move through each step successfully. For instance, Step 1 requires that there is a separation from the affair partner, but often times, a spouse will be resistant to letting that affair partner go. If this happens, you will want to read Chapter 9's section "When Your Partner Won't End the Affair" to address issues in that area. As you move from step to step, you can flip back-and-forth and troubleshoot if you approach problems along the way. Problems are expected, and this is why Chapter 9 is available to you. Use it as needed, and realize that it is part of the process though you might feel frustrated from time to time. Now let's move on to the 7 step plan!

Step 1
Right After Revealing the Betrayal

After finding out that your partner has cheated on you, your world splits apart. At this point, there are two relationships – the time before the affair and the time after. The innocence and safety that once existed in your relationship is gone and can never be reclaimed. Now this sounds extremely discouraging, but there is hope through the journey of healing. In fact, by going through the healing path, your relationship with your spouse will be stronger than ever. You are no longer trying to get your relationship back. Rather, you are creating a new one.

The betrayal of infidelity is so traumatic because your basic assumptions about what you thought existed in your monogamous relationship are broken. You might have assumed that you and your partner were exclusively committed to one another no matter what. You may have thought that both of you held the same moral values about monogamy. Doubt may never have been an issue when you thought about your partner, and now all you feel is doubt. Safety is gone and insecurity and pain are much of what you feel. You once thought your partner was trustworthy and honest, but now all of this is broken and you don't know what to believe, what you should do, or if you should stay.

At this point, you will be on a roller coaster ride of feelings. One day, you might feel that you want to reconcile, and another day, you might feel that you can never go on in this relationship. Accept that this will be a reality for the first three months of the relationship after you have discovered the betrayal.

Know that this roller coaster ride is a temporary one, and you will get to the point where you will establish safety. For now, use this time as a probationary period for the decision you will make later. Some days, you may not be able to muster any kind of caring for your partner. This is understandable. On those days, try to be as considerate and respectful as you can. At the very least, treat your partner as nicely as you would treat any stranger. You must be decent to one another to come through it on the other side in a better way.

How, What, When, and Where

You may want to have every question answered about the infidelity. Just understand that the answers must come in a helpful and controlled way. Understand that you do not need to know every detail of the affair. You deserve to know every detail if that is what you need for healing, and your partner will need to give that to you. For now, however, stick to basic questions – who, what, where, and when. This is what you need to know in the beginning stages and through a controlled and productive way. Do not burn the midnight oil staying up trying to work through all of the adulterous details. This will only intensify negative feelings and will be unproductive. You will need to set aside structured times for discussions.

If you feel that your emotions are completely out of whack, and you are feeling that you cannot control your anger, walk away or take a timeout. Try to avoid escalating arguments because they could result in even more damage to the relationship. Verbal or physical abuse can also happen in situations when escalated emotions occur. When in doubt, take a timeout.

Basically, what I want to show you is how to construct a process of disclosure that is productive and is not explosive. Because of this traumatic time in your life, it may be hard for you to act rationally and with self-control, but I am here to tell you that you can do it. If you are explosive and abusive because of the hurt that you feel, your partner will only pull away in fear of the consequences of your reactions. Your partner will not be forthcoming with the information that you need in order to heal if explosiveness is present. Even in this very early stage of the process, respect is essential and the road to understanding and improved commitment is much easier to complete.

In the beginning, you need questions answered. This is essential, of course. You need to understand the meaning of the infidelity and many of the details. Just stick to who, what, where, and when. For instance: How long has this infidelity been going on? When did the affair begin? When did you meet the affair partner when you were together sexually? Who else is aware of the affair? When was the last time that you were with your affair partner?

While these questions may be difficult to ask, and the answers may be even more difficult to hear, hearing the honest responses about the affair from your partner and what the relationship was like meets your basic need for information. Not every question needs to be answered at once because some questions will need to wait.

As agonizing as it might feel for you, the questions you might want to ask about why the affair happened and what it all meant need to come later in the process. These complex questions require a lot of thought and receptivity from both of you, and one or both of you may not be ready to reveal those answers or ready to hear them.

Pondering these questions and answers will only bring you more strife so it is better to leave them for later when both you and your partner are in a more receptive place. Stick to who, what, where, and when, and leave the "why" and "what does it all mean" questions for later.

Lastly, realize that you need to feel your feelings. This does not mean that you have to act on your feelings if those behaviors are destructive in any way. Remember, walk away when the anger gets to be too much or if it is too difficult to be around your partner at a certain time. Let your partner know that you might need periodic timeouts, and that you want to make this journey, as painful as it may be, a productive one. Again, treat one another as nicely as you would a stranger. Decency is the key here in order to have a productive healing process. Agree on this in the very beginning, and you will set a good foundation for upcoming recovery.

Confronting

You may be in a position where your partner has not discovered that you found out about the affair so you may need to confront your spouse. There is a productive way to do this and a destructive way to do this, as in all things, so continue to read on if you still need to confront your partner about the affair.

Before You Confront Your Partner

First and foremost, you need to know what you want to gain from the confrontation. Do you want your partner to acknowledge your suspicions? Do you want to ask your partner if working on the marriage is an option?

Figure out what you want to know so that you have clear communication when you have the confrontation discussion. After that, you can begin to think about whether you want to proceed forward working with your marriage or if you feel that you need to end it.

Be sure that you are open and honest about the confrontation. Avoid manipulation, hoping to ensnare your partner through devious ways. Ask your partner in a manner that is respectful and non-manipulative. You might want to say, "I have evidence about your affair, and I want you to tell me the truth about your affair." Avoid statements like, "So where were you last night?" Most importantly, stay calm. Give yourself time to calm down if you are not ready to approach your partner without aggressiveness. For you to be effective and gain as much honest feedback as you can, you must approach a partner with calmness and a low defensiveness.

If you are overly emotional, your partner will go on the defensive and will be less likely to offer honest information in fear of evoking more negative emotions in you. If you think that this will be the most difficult thing for you, write your thoughts down on a piece of paper so that you can be clear about what you want to say.

The Confrontation

When you are ready to confront your partner, choose a place where both of you are not distracted, and neither of you need to be anywhere. You want a time and place that is clear of distractions and excuses to flee. Confront in person. Do not confront via telephone, email, or text messaging. You need to have this discussion face-to-face.

When you discuss the affair, stick to the facts as you know them and avoid manipulation as I stated above. Discuss: What you know about the affair, What you might have seen, What you might have been told, and Any contradictions between what your partner has told you and what you discovered about the affair. Also, talk about how your partners' actions and lies make you feel. With that said, remember to be calm when you talk about your feelings of betrayal, sadness, fear, etc.

Realize that a typical reaction to a confrontation of infidelity is denial. Most partners will deny an affair and will try to find out what you might know first. When an admission occurs, that admission is usually not the whole story. Lying is also fairly typical. If your partner lies about the affair, it could be because your partner does not want to risk losing you or it may be because your partner may not be willing to give up the affair partner.

Stay calm, be patient, and stick to the facts. Remember that the What, When, Where, and Who questions are pertinent at this time. If your partner is honest with you through the confrontation, thank your partner for that honesty and let your partner know that you would rather know the truth about the affair than stay in the dark. If your partner refuses to admit to anything, continue to observe and trust your gut. Then, confront again.

It is common for partners to deny the affair, as I said. This is part of the process. Even if your partner eventually tells you the truth, denying initially and only giving half- truths will slow the process of healing. When the admissions are dragged out over a period of time, it is much more painful and difficult to heal. Quick attention to the trauma is key, if at all possible. Immediate honesty is always the best way to start the road to healing from infidelity.

Clean Breaks

For healing to begin, the affair partner must be completely out of the picture. All contact must be severed with that partner. What does this mean? Your spouse has to stop all personal contact with the affair partner. The spouse that has been having the affair must contact the affair partner and let that partner know that a commitment to rebuilding the marriage is a priority and that all communication will need to stop between the two of them. It must be very clear to everyone that the affair is over before healing and reparation of the relationship can begin. No phone calls, no meet ups, no emails, no text, you get the picture.

If there is a professional relationship with the affair partner, and that often does happen, then other tactics will need to be put into place because a clean break is not possible if both people cannot leave the professional relationship. So what if continued contact is unavoidable? I will tell you this; it will be more difficult when contact cannot be severed with the affair partner. When contact isn't severed completely, it creates additional stress on the relationship as the affair partner still continues to have a voice. However, in some instances contact is unavoidable.

If the affair partner is a coworker or something like that, first and foremost, contact needs to be limited to business matters only. The affair partner may still be in the picture because of a professional relationship, but the line in the sand needs to be clearly drawn. Boundaries are very important here. Going out for lunch together or talking personally about family life or even swapping stories about office gossip are inappropriate exchanges if a clear break is to be made.

Communication must be strictly for business purposes, and if the affair partner steers any conversation in a personal manner, your spouse needs to state, "I don't want to discuss that. Let's keep our relationship professional." Talking about your marriage is, of course, very inappropriate and the affair partner should know nothing about your relationship except for the fact that the affair has been severed.

In circumstances when encounters are unavoidable, such as work encounters, or even if the affair partner is seen in a certain area by surprise, those encounters need to be shared between spouses.

You and your partner must come to an agreement that any encounters with the affair partner will be communicated to one another. This is done to establish trust and safety. If your partner continues to be honest with you in every way possible, you will heal and establish safety much quicker. With that said, remember to remain calm and to be respectful when a disclosure happens.

The two of you will need to discuss how this sharing will happen. I find that it is helpful to establish a time to discuss the affair and any occurrences about the affair. You shouldn't be talking about it every day all day long because your partner will grow tired and defensive, and you will continue to be angry. Set a time aside each week for you to ask any questions about the affair and for your partner to be able to talk to you about affair topics. The scheduled times are mostly for you to ask questions. Agree with your partner that all unavoidable encounters will be discussed openly and that you will hold up your end of the deal that you will remain calm and respectful.

You may need a safe space to do this, which is why I mention appropriate times set aside for this. By having this agreement, your partner is more likely to volunteer the information, and you are less likely to have to pry it out through interrogation.

Step 2
Discuss the Affair

Rather than staying silent and sitting with your feelings of insecurity or anger, it is more helpful to discuss your feelings and ask questions of your partner and allow your partner to help you through this difficult process.

If you are feeling angry, let your partner know. This goes the same for feeling hurt, insecure, and a whole range of other emotions. In addition to talking about your feelings, you will have lots of questions that will come up for you, and your partner will be the only person that can answer those questions. On that note, realize that your partner wants everything to go away and for the two of you to start fresh. This is impossible as you need to go through the healing process and feel your feelings about being betrayed in such a way. So what do you do?

Pummeling your partner with questions day after day as they come up is a poor strategy because your partner will inevitably keep running away and defensiveness will be the result. You will feel even more frustrated and betrayed, and your partner will feel frustrated as well. Whatever you need to know to heal, you will need to ask of your partner. However, you need to approach your spouse in a better way so that your partner will be more receptive to your questions.

Understand that the questions that you have for your partner will come in waves, and it will be tempting to ask about everything as questions pop up for you. Refrain from doing this. Instead, write down your questions in your journal. Set up an hour session with your partner once or twice a week so that you can ask any question that you like in that meeting. In this meeting, you will ask the questions that you have written down as they have come to you, and your partner will answer those questions. After the hour is over, the meeting is over and no more questions should be asked until the next meeting. What this does is allows your partner to have a break from consistent questions coming day to day, and it gives you a receptive partner who answers your questions during your meeting.

I have found that the couples that I work with find this strategy very helpful. In many cases, a weekly meeting is not always needed and the entire hour is not needed either. Because both partners are receptive and open to the process, a lot of information is exchanged and a couple can move forward throughout the week healing in different ways.

Whenever you have the scheduled meetings for you to ask questions about the affair, make an agreement that you will listen without attacking your partner. Your partner needs to know that the answers given in the sessions will not result in emotional repercussions for the rest of the week or in the session. The sessions are meant for information exchange, and while you may have negative feelings as you gain information, remember that respect is key here. Restrain negative reactions such as lashing out. If you find that you are unable to control your emotions, agree with your partner that in those instances, you will need to take a timeout and walk away.

If both of you agree to terms that are productive, the process will be much easier to go through. Throughout these meetings, remember that your partner is the healer. Your partner needs to reassure you throughout this process that both of you are committed to working on the relationship. This brings us to the next step, asking for reassurance.

Step 3
Reassurance & Guiding the Way

Throughout your journey of healing, you will have good days and bad days. On some days you will feel hopeful and strong, and on other days you will feel doubt and sadness.

On many of these occasions, insecurity will be an overwhelming emotion. You may wonder if your partner really loves you or what you did wrong to make your partner stray. While many of your feelings may not speak to the truth, you will still have them and will blame yourself on many occasions.

Asking for Reassurance

You will need a lot of reassurance from your partner as you rebuild your marriage. Make your partner aware that his or her role in reassuring you is an essential part of healing your relationship because it is essential to feel reassured while rebuilding trust.

Let your partner know that you will have some low days and on those days, you will ask for reassurances. Refrain from accusations and lashing out at your partner on the days that you feel low as these behaviors will only create defensiveness.

Both of you should have an agreement; you will continue to be respectful when emotions are low, and your partner will reassure you when you ask for it. Do not assume that your partner will have great days every day as your partner will also have some low days and may need some patience from you. The way that you ask for reassurance is correlated with the response that you get. If you attack, you will get a defensive response. Instead of saying, "I know that you don't love me anymore because you cheated on me." Say something like, "I am feeling pretty low today, and I would like some feedback about your feelings for me to make me feel better." There are even more strategies for working together in Step 7, and you also have the troubleshooting pointers so read this book to the end for all of the information to come together for you.

Even though your spouse needs to be the healer in these situations, you have to guide the way. Basically, you have to teach your spouse what you need in terms of reassurances. Identify what works for you, and give that feedback to your spouse. For instance, it may be really helpful when your spouse calls you several times from work. Let your spouse know that so this can happen for you.

Better yet, make a list of the things that work so that you can let your partner know how to reassure you during your low points. The more specific you are about the help you need, the more help you will get from your partner. Both of you want to heal from this affair, and this is what you are both working towards. The goal is the same for both of you so do not work against one another; work together. This is done through concrete instructions and feedback about what is working and what isn't.

During your scheduled times when you are asking questions about the affair, you might also use those times to give your spouse feedback about what you need for reassurances.

As you talk together during those times, you will find that you will need less and less time to have these particular meetings.

You Must Guide the Way

The most effective way to enable someone else to change is to get that person to do more or less of a behavior that is working or isn't working. That is, you must reinforce that person's behaviors so that the person is doing what you want. This is your role, while your spouse is the healer, you are the leader, and you'll need strategies to lead effectively.

In addition to the weekly meetings that I mentioned before, you will also need to work on your marriage day to day. If you are the only one reading this book, this means that you will be the one making the behavioral changes first. If your spouse is also reading this book, your spouse can make changes just as you make changes. However, it only takes one person to get changes moving in the right direction so do not be discouraged if you are acting alone at this point. With that said, you will be leading the way on many occasions so get comfortable with asking for what you need.

The first step of guiding your way through healing is to make a list of the needs that you have. You already have your needs of reassurances so here are some more ideas to get you started on other things you might require so that you feel safe in your marriage:

- Your spouse must make a clean break with the affair partner

- Your partner should respond when you ask for reassurances

- Both of you will attend weekly meetings to discuss any questions you might have about the affair

- Construction of an Internet policy at home – Internet must be used in a common area in the home if online love affairs have been a problem

- You spouse should volunteer information if there has been any contact with the affair partner

- Your partner should call you several times during the work day.

Approaching your partner with your list of needs will take some finesse, and the way that you approach your partner will depend on the reaction you receive. Here are some tips on approaching in an effective manner. These are also tips for helping you through many hard times because your partner may not always behave in a way that's helpful to you. That might also be the case for your reactions so both of you can use these general techniques to turn things around when things get tough.

Expect the Best

When you expect that your spouse will fail or that defeat is imminent before you tackle a challenging situation, failure is usually the result. Ask yourself how you would handle something differently if you were expecting a positive outcome instead. How might your approach to your spouse be different if you thought that your spouse would respond in a positive way rather than a defensive way?

If you knew you would get a loving response, how would you approach your spouse in the first place? Once you determine how you would act in such a situation, act as if this will happen. Expect the best outcome. Pretend that things will turn out in a positive way, and approach the situation in that way.

If you expect a defensive and angry response, you would approach your partner in a negative and defensive manner, wouldn't you? Well, what if you approached in a manner that was expectant of a positive response? I will tell you, you will get a different response from your partner.

To get the process started, in your journal, ask yourself these questions:

1. Normally, how would I approach the situation if I was looking at it negatively?

2. What would I like the situation to be instead?

3. If I were expecting positive results, how would I approach the situation differently?

After you have asked yourself these questions, expect that you will get positive results. Do everything you would do if you were convinced that things will turn out in a positive manner, and you will definitely get different outcomes.

Change Your Approach

We are all habitual beings, and most of the time, we interact in the same ways time after time. We engage in expected behaviors and continue to do the same things over and over again while anticipating different results. For example, a spouse may nag her partner to take out the trash every day, and consistently, her partner continues to ignore her.

Even though the nagging is not working, the wife continues with the same behavior expecting that her husband will listen. He doesn't. Both partners become frustrated, and nothing is solved. Avoid this. Think about what you would normally do, and do something different.

In your journal, write down some of the behaviors that you engage in to try to get your partner to do things. Perhaps you nag your partner, as I mentioned in the example. Perhaps you are an overbearing cheerleader when your spouse is feeling down, and your spouse gets frustrated. These are just a few examples for you to start thinking about your behaviors.

When you are writing in your journal, be specific when you describe your behaviors. For example, if you tend to be suspicious because your partner is away from the house longer than you feel your partner should be, discuss what you concretely do in these situations. Do you meet your spouse at the door when he returns home and ask him where he's been? Do you ignore your spouse when he returns from home and continue to ignore him for the rest of the night?

When you identify your unproductive behaviors, do something differently when your spouse comes home. For example, if you tend to ask a million questions when your spouse returns home, you might engross yourself in an activity and have him find you in the house. You might refrain from asking any questions and just greet your spouse with a "hello." You get the point.

In your journal, ask yourself this:

1. What behavior do I engage in when my spouse does this (add partner's behavior here)?

2. What are some things I could do that would be different from what I have been doing that would surprise my spouse?

Continue to change your behavior as you receive the responses that you desire from your partner, and stick with those instead of doing more of the same unproductive behaviors.

Do the Opposite

Something that you're doing doesn't work; try doing the exact opposite of that. It may sound strange, but it is effective quite often. Because we get stuck in our patterns, we continue to do the same thing over and over again, and we continue to get the same negative results. Turning things around and doing the *complete opposite* results in different behaviors from the other person. Give it a try.

I worked with a client who was struggling with his wife who was depressed. I asked him what he usually did when she got down, and he said that he would tell her it would get better and would also give her information about therapists who would be able to help her. Although his exchanges with her came from a helpful place, he was not helping her or himself.

She grew more frustrated with him and sunk deeper into her depression. I told him to do the exact opposite of what he had been doing. I told him to not say anything until she brought it up, and when she did start talking about how depressed she was, instead of cheerleading and instead of suggesting helpful interventions, he should just agree with her.
He could tell her that he was also concerned but maybe this was the way that she was and that she might not ever get better.

I told him that he should also tell her that he will have to focus on himself when she gets into a depressive state and take care of what he needs to take care of for himself because he didn't see any way of helping her. Even though this interaction was completely unnatural to him, he stated that he would give it a try.

In the next session, he told me that his wife started talking about her depression and how awful she felt, and he did the opposite of what he had always done (which was cheerleading and suggesting). Sure enough, she completely changed her attitude that very day. All of a sudden, she was more upbeat and she was convinced and determined to prove to him and herself that she could get out of her rut. She attended a local yoga class the next day, which had been something that she never even considered prior to this "change" in her husband's attitude.

In doing the opposite, my client helped his spouse act in ways that were more productive. He realized that she grew more and more depressed as he continued to cheer her on, and although he knew it wasn't working, he felt that there was no other way. It felt strange to him to do the complete opposite of what he had been doing, but as you can see, the results are always different when you change your behaviors.

In your situation, think of something that you do with your spouse that breeds negative results time after time even though you want positive results. When you have that behavior in mind, write it down in your journal. Then think of what the opposite of that behavior would be. What will you do instead? When you have identified this behavior, give it a try next time the opportunity arises. Observe the results, and write them down in your journal.

Keep track of the techniques that you try and what is working, and read about them in your journal when you are feeling frustrated or when you are feeling that progress is slow. Often, we think that positive progress is coincidental and not indicative of what we are doing.

Keeping the journal helps you take note of the strategies you have been trying and the results that you have been getting, as small as they may seem. This is important because it's easy to lose track of specifics when you are living with someone day to day. You'll need the written reminders to keep facts straight.

Remember that all of these techniques are used through trial and error. Sometimes a behavior may work and sometimes it may not. This is another reason why it's important to note things in your journal – so that you can keep track of them and tweak your behaviors as needed.

You will use these techniques in your relationship even after you both heal from the infidelity. They will be helpful for both of you for years to come. Pay close attention to your progress and, before you know it, you'll be a pro at turning things around.

Step 4
Identify Reasons for the Affair

It certainly is tempting to compare your relationship to your partner's affair. However, keep in mind that comparing these two relationships is like comparing apples and oranges. It's like looking at reality vs. idealism (or even fantasy).

You would be comparing what it would feel like to be in a reality-based long-term relationship (your marriage) as opposed to being in a romantic relationship that is idealized and short term (the affair). The affair would always win.

The affair did not happen because the affair partner is somehow better than you. Take that out of your mind. If you're asking yourself, "What is wrong with me? Why does the affair partner have that I don't have?" you could drive yourself crazy. Comparing your relationship to the affair relationship is unrealistic and unhealthy. With that said, you do need to identify reasons for why the affair happened so that you and your partner will not repeat mistakes made in the past. This is not to say that the affair was your fault, but obviously the relationship needed some work. There is a reason your partner strayed, and starting to identify those reasons is essential.

Realize that in most cases, what attracts you to your partner can end up being a problem later. This is also the case for your spouse and the affair partner. Just because the affair partner looked like a better option at some point for your spouse, the traits that attracted your spouse to the affair partner would probably end up being problems in the long-term.

If your spouse left you for the affair partner, in many cases, the cycle of moving from one relationship to the next would result because destructive patterns would, most likely, occur again. So don't beat yourself up over that. Don't think that somehow, you must be defective or not good enough. That just simply isn't true. Many spouses choose an affair partner that is the exact opposite from their long-term partner because they are looking for something different to jerk them out of their discontent.

Finding a partner with opposite traits than a partner in a problematic marriage may sound like a solution (and isn't that why affairs happen in the first place?), but this solution is temporary because as the affair relationship continues, those opposite traits end up being liabilities for your spouse.

In many cases, an affair is a nice place to visit, but your partner may not want to live there on a permanent basis. All of this information is to let you know that your relationship with your partner is not substandard to the affair relationship so when you start to feel bad about yourself, remember this information.

Reasons for the Affair

When you discuss the reasons for the affair with your partner, use the meeting strategy you used for asking questions about your partner's affair. If you choose, set aside the same time and place as you did for the questions meeting. At this point, you may be finished talking about the details of the affair, but you will still need to discuss the reasons for affair so this is a good time for this transition.

If you still need questions meetings, separate the questions meeting and the reasons meeting during the week or the focus of the meeting will get too muddled with two agendas.

Discuss reasons for the affair only within the scheduled time just as you did for posing questions about the details of the affair. If you continue to talk about reasons for the affair as they come up for you in your mind, your partner will inevitably start fleeing. Understand that your partner may not be able to initially identify why the affair happened. This is very common.

Whether or not your partner can identify why the affair happened, it still helps to have these conversations and to discover the reasons together. Following is a list of the most common reasons why people have affairs so that you can have some discussion points for your meetings. Remember to remain calm, and remember to be respectful just as you have continued to be through your questions meetings.

Your partner, most likely, had an affair because he or she was looking for emotional or physical connection somewhere else. In your relationship, something was lacking, and your partner chose to step out of the relationship and fill that void with somebody else. Whether it was unintentional (perhaps it was a friendly work relationship that crossed boundaries into a physical affair) or if it was blatantly intentional (maybe your partner put an ad out online to meet someone), either way, a void was being filled.

The reasons below are common voids in relationships that people try to fill with outside relationships rather than trying to bridge the gap within their current relationships.

Common Reasons for Affairs

- Feeling as if a partner is taking you for granted
- Feeling criticized by one's partner
- An inadequate sex life
- Low self-esteem and limited ego boost within the relationship
- Boredom
- Sexual addiction
- Midlife crisis

- One bad decision, such as getting drunk and having a one night stand
- Mental health issues, like Bipolar Disorder

While you are having these discussions, continue to be respectful and walk away and take a timeout if you need. Throughout these "reasons for the affair meetings," it will be difficult to hear your partner's replies, but it is necessary feedback, and the information will only serve your marriage in the future if you both learn from it. Once you are able to identify the reason or reasons for the affair, both of you can work together to bridge the gap and fill the void in your relationship or, in some cases, you may need to seek professional help for certain issues such as addictions and disorders.

In other cases, you may come to a dead end. You may not be able to identify together why the affair happened as sometimes it is a more complex question that needs to be answered. Even after discussing all of the minute details of the affair and what has been dissatisfactory in a marriage, a couple can fail to come up with an answer to Why? In other cases, you may come up with some answers, but the answer may feel incomplete or not reason enough. For instance, many partners say that they were curious and this is why they had the affair. For obvious reasons, this reasoning is not satisfactory to the partner that has been betrayed as we are *all* curious at times.

If you find that you and your partner come to a dead-end on finding the reasons for the affair, ask what explanations for the infidelity *do not* apply. Make a list with each sentence starting, "I did not have an affair because…" In these instances, you and your partner may be able to start moving forward in this way.

While your partner may not be able to give you a direct answer to the question, "Why?" giving explanations for why the infidelity *did not* apply to your partner is a different step in the same direction.

While these scheduled meetings will be difficult, they serve a twofold purpose. First and foremost, you structure a healing space so that the hurt from the affair does not encompass every day in your and your partner's life.

Second, you are forced to work together during these meetings. When you and your partner achieve your goals together and solve problems together, there is a mutual respect and affection that develops. You are both putting your relationship ahead of all other distractions and obligations so you and your partner form a united front and dedicate yourselves to working on your relationship together. Think of how powerful this is, especially since an affair is such a splintering process.

By working together through the hurt and discussing reasons for the affair and past problems in your relationship, you and your partner achieve a bond. By continuing these meetings, you are putting your relationship first, and you are fighting against the splintering process of the affair. Having a shared meaning about the infidelity is a core element for recovery.

Step 5
Managing Flashbacks and Obsessions

After you found out about your partner's affair, you probably felt a whole range of feelings including shock, anger, hurt, sadness, confusion, and disbelief. At times, it still may feel as if you cannot make it through the day.

These emotions are normal because of what you are going through, and you should expect these feelings. You may feel anger at one moment and then a few minutes later, you might feel devastation or intense sadness. In one moment, you may feel neutral and then rage about what happened. You may cry a lot and find it difficult to function throughout the day. Your sleep may also be disturbed.

Understand that in these beginning stages, after you have found out about the affair, your feelings will seem like they are controlling you. While this is completely normal, you can manage your feelings, and they do not have to rule your days. Having said this, it is also important to note that you do need to experience many of your feelings and push through them rather than avoid them. Many of the techniques are for fully feeling your feelings and other techniques are for redirecting feelings.

Use these techniques as appropriate. For example, you may be at work and feelings of intense sadness may hit you. At that moment, it would be inappropriate for you to take time out to feel the sadness and push through that sadness as you are on paid time and your employer is paying you to do your job. So in these instances, I provide you with techniques to help you redirect feelings so that you can go about your day.

In other instances, you may have time to experience your feelings and process them appropriately while feeling sadness or hurt, and I give you techniques to do that too. In addition, while this step can be done independently, remember that it is also important to discuss your feelings with your partner and allow your partner to help you through this painful process.

If you have worked through the previous steps with your partner, I would assume that talking about your feelings with one another has already been going on so keep that up. When feelings are too overwhelming and you want to lash out, take a timeout. Here are some strategies you can use during the timeout:

Journal Work

Writing down your thoughts provides an outlet for letting things go. Basically, when you write your thoughts and emotions down on paper, your brain is no longer cluttered with racing thoughts, and those thoughts and feelings are left on the paper. It is also a safe way to express yourself and explore different thoughts and feelings without concerning yourself with what effect they might have on others.

Write in an uncensored way, and follow your emotions and obsessions until you feel that everything is out. In this way, you can also discover new things and come to clarifications about thoughts that might have confused you before you had written them down.

When you start to obsess because of negative emotions that come up for you due to the betrayal, pull out your journal and write whenever the mood strikes you. You can use the computer, but I always recommend using paper and pen. There's something about the physical act of handwriting that is healing and allows you to let things out more effectively. Also, digital data is prone to being discovered or hacked, and while this may not be a huge concern for you, it is something to take into account.

In your journal, you can also write in a letter format. You can write a letter to your partner or you can even write a letter to the affair partner in an uncensored way.

Just let your feelings flow out on paper, and let that letter stay in your journal. The letter is not intended to be mailed or to be given away to anybody, but it is a way for you to be able to speak to the person that has hurt you without censorship. Again, this is a way for *you* to release your thoughts and feelings so that they are not cluttering your mind. You can also write a list of questions every time you feel overwhelmed with unanswered questions about the affair. This exercise has a twofold benefit: It allows you to free your mind of obstruction, and it also gives you a list of questions to discuss during your next meeting with your spouse.

Guided Meditation

Meditation is a wonderful way to release stress and work through obsessions. There is one guided meditation in particular that is very effective for dealing with negative emotions. This meditation exercise helps you feel the intensity of the pain and then lets you experience the process of letting go. This is a very effective and powerful exercise, and I encourage you to use it when you have an opportunity to do so. In some cases, you will not have the time or the space to engage in this meditation so there are a few other techniques you can use. However, when you can, make the time to go through the guided meditation because it is incredibly powerful.

"Facing and Letting Go" Meditation

Find a calm and silent place where you can be alone with your thoughts. Close your eyes and focus on one especially negative thought.

Make that negative thought bigger and bigger, and really feel the pain caused by that thought. Let that thought surround you. Imagine that it has a color and a shape, and make that thought, now with color and shape, a physical entity surrounding you. Look at the color and look at the shape of that negative thought all around you. Feel it all around you. Where do you feel it in your body? Focus in on it. Feel the oppression and the negativity of that thought. Let yourself sit in it and let it overwhelm you.

Next, focus on the shape and the color of that thought and visualize it getting smaller and smaller. Slowly, imagine that it is getting even smaller until that shape and color of that negative thought fits into the palm of your hand. Once it fits into the palm of your hand, place it in between your thumb and your index finger, and visualize it getting smaller. As you press down on that thought with your fingers, visualize that thought becoming miniscule. As it becomes smaller and smaller, imagine that it is almost invisible. Once it becomes the size of a grain of sand, throw it as far away as you can.

Visualize it soaring over the ocean. Visualize it soaring in the air and falling down over the horizon until you can no longer see it. Now tune into your feeling state.

How do you feel? Do you feel peaceful? Do you feel relieved? If the negative emotion has disappeared, sit in the stillness and enjoy the calm. Think of the positive things in your life that come up for you or you can just feel the pleasure of the stillness in the moment.

If the negativity hasn't moved away, begin again with making it bigger and then smaller until you can throw it away over the ocean. Extend the times of visualizing each negative thought longer than before. Keep practicing when you have the still time and place to use this meditation. It's powerful.

Creating Anchors

In this exercise, you will create a touch anchor that you can use on yourself when negative thoughts are overwhelming you. The point of this exercise is to have an anchor that gives you a shot of positivity when you need it. You can use anchors whether you are alone or in a crowded room so it is very handy.

The Technique

To create your anchor, use your non-dominant hand for this activity – so if you are right-handed you would use your left hand and vice a versa. With the tip of your thumb, find a spot on the second knuckle of your middle finger. Touch that for a while. This spot is going to be your touch anchor that we are going to create.

Now, think of a time in your past when you felt very optimistic and hopeful. It could be anything, but I would suggest using something that is non-relationship related since it would be a less complicated visualization (considering most of your obsessive thoughts are due to the relationship process). Your optimistic and hopeful memory could be a time when you graduated high school or when your first child was born. Maybe it was when you took a hike on a vacation you had with your family. Perhaps you had a hopeful and optimistic feeling when you won a track meet or finished a difficult project at work.

Take a moment now, and think of that memory that made you feel optimistic and positive. Remember that memory vividly. Experience it and relive it. Enjoy that moment. Really stay in that moment and feel the optimism and happiness and the confidence. Do this for about 30 seconds.

Think about what you were seeing at the time. Notice what your body felt like and what you were wearing. When you reach the peak of feeling good, touch your thumb to that inside knuckle once.

Now go back to that memory and notice the feeling again. After you have felt that feeling again, think of a different memory when you felt good or even better than the previous memory. Imagine this new experience in the same way that you imagined the last experience. What did you feel? What were you wearing, and how did your body feel? Think of it as if you were in a photograph or in a movie. Visualize all of it in your mind. Now go further, and actually be yourself in that moment, and experience that moment again. Whenever you have reached the peak of feeling good, touch your thumb to be inside second knuckle of your middle finger again once.

Now imagine that positive feeling being twice as strong. What would that feel like? How does your body feel? As you imagine the feeling being twice as strong, touch the tip of your thumb to your middle knuckle again once. Now *double* that feeling as you touch the tip of your thumb to your middle knuckle. Imagine that feeling now.

Now take a break, and stop what you are doing. Look around you and stay in the moment of now. At this point, you will be back to your normal feeling of today. Now think of your phone number and say it backwards. After this, touch your thumb to your middle knuckle again and notice any good feelings that arise. You should feel that elated feeling that you anchored. Feel it? Pretty neat, right?

Now you have a physical anchor that you can use when you are at work and feeling negative thoughts or in a place where you are unable to journal or meditate. To strengthen your anchor, continue to think of positive memories that gave you feelings of happiness and confidence, and touch your middle finger to your thumb to anchor.

This is called stacking, and will continue to make that anchor stronger as you do this so that you can use it when you need it. Next time you need to feel good in a tight situation, you have the anchor to help.

Managing Flashbacks

Flashbacks will be part of the healing process and while they are frustrating, they are completely normal. Through your healing journey, the flashbacks will become weaker, and eventually, they will be only twinges of pain rather than full painful re-experiences, and that will be how you will know you are making progress. Some flashbacks happen because there might have been an event during the time you discovered the affair. For instance, you might have been watching a certain television program when you discovered your partner was unfaithful, and anytime that program is mentioned, you have a painful flashback about the affair. A flashback is always sudden and always painful. You can cope with instances such as these in a few different ways depending on the situation:

Predicting – some flashbacks will be predictable because they might happen every time a certain events occurs. A certain television program may produce a flashback for you. One woman found out about her husband's affair during Thanksgiving so when she watched the Macy's Thanksgiving Day Parade, she suffered flashbacks.

If you have an event that is a predictable flashback, "write over" the memory with something reparative. For instance, you can imprint a new memory.

You could have your partner watch the parade with you to create or go to your family's house and create a new tradition around the Macy's Thanksgiving Day Parade broadcast if it is something that is important to you.

You can always choose to avoid the situation, but if it isn't something you want to omit out of your life, "writing over" an experience with something more positive is a good way to avoid a predictable flashback in the future.

Avoidance – of course, many flashbacks are not predictable, but you can learn to avoid trigger situations. For instance, if a certain route from work gives you a flashback from time to time because, perhaps, there is a trigger along the way, you may want to create a new route from work to avoid negative feelings.

You may not have to drive that new route the entire time you are working there, but in the beginning, it may be better to avoid certain triggers to decrease the emotional turmoil. As you heal, certain triggering routines may no longer be a problem and won't need to be avoided anymore.

Proceed with Feeling – in some occasions, you may not be able to avoid or predict a flashback, and a negative emotion will come flooding towards you. Expect this, and if you can, feel that feeling fully. Depending on the situation you are in, you may be able to manage it with the techniques I have outlined previously, but if you can't, do not block it, and just feel the feeling. Remember that a feeling is like a wave, and it will pass. This negative feeling will not last forever, just like a craving for a drug, it will decrease and eventually go away.

Let yourself feel it. Better yet, experience the negative feeling just like the way I discussed in the meditation exercise, but in an abbreviated way if necessary. It will pass, and you will be stronger when you come out on the other side.

In time, as you heal from the infidelity, and as you and your partner become stronger, flashbacks will occur less often, and they will be much weaker. As you move through the healing process, things will become easier, and forgiveness will also come.

Step 6
Forgiveness

Forgiveness is a process rather than a single action. Throughout your healing journey, you have probably done some forgiving already. Forgiveness comes after some healing has taken place and after some trust has been re-established. Demanding forgiveness right after the betrayal is unrealistic and does not speak to the suffering that occurred.

As you continue through the healing process and safety is established more and more, you will let go of some anger, and this is good. As you and your partner are healing together, you are both gaining some empathy for one another's situations. You do not need to forgive at first, but eventually, it is essential if you and your partner are to have a successful and fulfilling relationship.

As you move closer towards the end of the 7 step healing process, it will be the right time to discuss a conscious choice to forgive. If you are ready to take the steps, you are at the end of your healing journey. At this point, there should be no additional surprises or epiphanies about the affair if you are to move forward to forgiving.

What Forgiveness Is Not

Forgiveness is not forgetting about what happened or pretending that the affair didn't happen. It is not an excuse for the affair, and it is not the act of condoning your partner's past behaviors. Forgiveness is also not a permission to continue destructive behavior. It is also not reconciliation. If you choose to move on from your relationship, you can still forgive and will need to forgive in order to heal yourself. You can choose to forgive your partner and let go of any feelings of revenge but know that reconciliation is not on the menu.

Forgiveness Defined

Forgiveness, essentially, is something for you. If you are to free yourself from all of the burdensome feelings of the past, you have to forgive the person who wronged you. In forgiveness, you will be able to move forward in your life and have a more productive and happy journey. Forgiveness is a choice. It is your choice to forgive someone, and if you choose to forgive, you are stating that you will no longer be a prisoner to past betrayals.

Forgiveness is also a process, and it will take some time. It is dependent on the remorse of your partner. Forgiveness needs to involve both of you because it is a commitment to one another. In forgiving, you allow yourself to let go of the pain, the obsessions, the bitterness, and the resentment towards your partner. You no longer need to punish your partner because forgiveness lets you release that need. In return, your partner must show you true remorse and must be able to demonstrate an understanding of the pain that he or she has put you through.

When it is Not Appropriate to Forgive

If the offending behavior has not stopped by your partner, forgiveness is not a possibility. If your partner is not remorseful or does not take responsibility for what has happened, forgiveness is not appropriate. Apologies and change both need to happen in order for forgiveness to take place. For example, if your partner has made many apologies and is truly remorseful but continues to engage in hurtful behaviors, you are not in a position to forgive. If your partner continues to act in hurtful ways because he or she has mental health issues or addiction issues, there is some reading for you to do in Chapter 9.

Forgiving Too Soon

Be aware, that it is a mistake to forgive too soon. If you have not worked through the pain and anger, you may not be ready to forgive just yet. You need to feel that you are in a position of safety and increased trust, and your partner needs to show true remorse along with behavioral changes. Forgiveness is a team effort in this sense. Also, if you have any lingering suspicions that your partner is still doing some unfaithful things, forgiveness should not be addressed at this point. Again, you cannot move forward, and you cannot forgive your partner if you do not feel safe.

Are You Ready to Forgive?

You may also want to look at yourself too. You may have difficulty moving beyond your anger and frustration if you are in a victim mind set. Maybe you cannot move past the betrayal and feel like your partner has ruined your life.

Perhaps you are unwilling to let go of the anger despite your partner's best efforts to make things right. In this case, ask yourself if your partner has shown enough behavioral modifications to gain your trust. Do you feel safe? Has your partner shown you that he or she is committed to working on the relationship? Are you scared that your partner is still carrying on the affair? If you answered no to the first two questions and yes to the third, you might want to ask yourself if you are stuck in a victim role. Are you punishing your partner despite the changes your partner has made? Be brutally honest with yourself. What is the evidence that keeps you unsure and unable to forgive?

How Do I Forgive?

It is easier to forgive if your spouse understands how much hurt you have been through due to the betrayal and wants to help make the pain go away. If you have seen positive behavioral changes in your partner, and you feel that your partner is truly remorseful, you are on your way to granting forgiveness. Here is how:

1) First and foremost, you need to acknowledge your pain and talk about your feelings with your partner without yelling or accusing.

2) Be aware that this is difficult for your partner as well. Because your partner is still held accountable for your pain, it is a vulnerable situation to be in. However, at this point, the anger has subsided because you have more compassion for your partner's vulnerabilities.

3) Now this is important. Be very specific about what you will and will not put up with. There are some things in your life moving forward that can be negotiated, but you must decide what those things are and tell your partner that you can't forgive as long as certain needs are met. For instance, there needs to be a clean break from the affair partner, and you may have some stipulations depending on the situation – perhaps your spouse works with the affair partner.

4) Be very specific about what you are forgiving. You want your partner to understand that you are aware of your partner's regrets, and be specific about those regrets and that you are forgiving them. This creates clarity and understanding between the two of you.

5) Seal the deal with something that shows forgiveness verbally, physically, or in writing. You might want to give your spouse a hug and a kiss after you have granted forgiveness, for example. You might want to give a card with some of your thoughts inside. There are many options so do what comes naturally to you.

6) Lastly, after you have granted your partner forgiveness, let go of blame and accusations. From this point forward, it is time to enjoy the freedom of letting go of past regrets. You won't forget (as the memories of the hard times are the very memories that teach us lessons to make our relationships better), but you should fully forgive.

Step 7
Keeping Positive Changes Going

If you have arrived at this step, it means that you have made substantial changes in your relationship, and you want to keep those positive changes going. Congratulations! As you have worked through these steps, you have had your ups and downs, and I'm sure the journey has not been easy. I know that it's difficult to appreciate how far you and your partner have come from the day the affair was uncovered. Many days, you might feel frustrated and feel that this healing journey is too much work. This is why it is important to see the entire picture and all the progress you and your partner have made.

Examining Progress

Ask yourself the following questions to find out where you are in your relationship right now and where you want to be in the future:

Prior to working through the 7 Step Plan, where would you have rated your relationship on a scale of 1 to 10? (1 means that it was the worst relationship you had ever been in, and 10 means that your relationship was perfect and needs no more improvement.)

1. On this 10 point scale, where is your relationship right now?

2. After you have rated your relationship on the scale, ask yourself this question: "Am I satisfied with where my relationship is right now?"

3. If you are dissatisfied, where would you like to be on the scale of 1 to 10? (Remember that no marriage is perfect so a score of 10 is usually unrealistic.)

4. Now ask yourself, what can I do to increase the number on the scale? Work slowly – if you are at a 6, how would you get to a 6 ½?

After you have answered these questions, you can also ask your partner to answer these questions. You will then learn how to address these issues using Maintenance Meetings so that you can keep the positive changes going in your relationship. Discuss your progress during those meetings. Remember to be respectful, calm, and understanding on both sides.

If you and your partner feel that there are still some things to work on, here are some guidelines for discussing your progress and the changes you feel you still need to make:

1) Look at the progress that you have already made and be grateful to one another for how far you have come. Even if you've only come a short distance, improvements are always to be celebrated. I hope you and your partner find encouragement from looking at your progress even though you both might feel that you still have quite a way to go in your relationship.

2) Identify what goals you both need to meet so that the next few weeks or months will be productive. First, write down both of your progress ratings and then ask yourselves the question again:

What are one or two things we can do that would bring our relationship satisfaction up half a point on the scale?

When you think of strategies to improve your relationship, think in behavioral and measurable terms. You must be able to see evidence of progress through observable results. For example,

- In order for us to move half a point up on the scale, I need to daily tell my partner that I love him or her.

- My partner will initiate spending more quality time together.

- We need to continue to have our weekly meeting on Saturday morning for one hour.

- My partner needs to check in with me if work is running late by giving me a call.

- When I'm feeling insecure, I will ask my partner for reassurance.

After you and your partner have identified the goals, discuss what you think and feel about your plan moving forward, and write down a date and time to meet again so that you can discuss your ongoing progress. Perhaps you and your partner feel that two months is a sufficient amount of time to implement your behavioral changes and assess progress again. Write the meeting time down in your journal and on the calendar for both of you to see so that you both can have it on the agenda for that next meeting you schedule.

Troubleshooting

During your goal-setting and goal-implementing process, you and your partner may hit some rough patches. You might trigger your partner's hot buttons because of something you are doing, and progress may lag because of it. Your partner might feel discouraged for a few days because of something going on at work, and you might feel insecure because of the distance you feel. Remember Step 3? Go back to that step, and read it through again. Identify the things that you need to change in your behavior to help things along so that you and your partner are working better together.

You may need to ask for reassurance or you may need to take a timeout when things get too overwhelming. You may need to stop doing something that isn't working despite your best efforts. Also, remember that this journey is a process, and it will take some trial and error. You might feel frustrated at times. Sometimes relationships get difficult because one or both partners have regressed or paused instead of moving forward with positive behavioral changes. That happens. All you have to do is correct the situation from that point on. If there is something you have been doing that hasn't been working, remember what has worked, and do that instead. Step 3 is there to guide your way so reread that whenever you need help.

It might be the case that you have tried a number of behaviors to turn things around and you haven't seen results. In the following list, there are a few steps that you can take if you feel that nothing is changing despite your making the behavioral changes outlined in Step 3.

1) **Not Enough Time** – it could be that you have not given the technique a sufficient amount of time. While it may feel like it is unproductive,

try to give it a little bit more time for a week or two until it is clear that the behavior you are implementing is not effective. Once you determine that, quit that and try something different.

2) **Too Similar** – sometimes you might be trying a different behavior, but the behavior you are trying is too similar to what you've already been doing. You might, in fact, be trying a different variation of the same technique. For example, if you are always nagging your spouse about something your spouse needs to change, and you decide that instead, you will ask him or her nicely, the result might be the same. It may be that the sheer act of asking your partner to do something, no matter how nicely, produces a negative response. Doing something different would be not asking at all, for example. Figure out for yourself, when you try something new, is the behavior really new or is it just a variation of something that you've done before that hasn't worked?

3) **Overlooking Signs of Change** – when you feel frustrated that changes are not occurring for you in your relationship, it may be that you are overlooking small signs of positive change. This is really easy to do and quite common. Because you want your relationship to be better, you feel frustrated at the progress you have made because, when you consider the progress scale, you want to be at a 9 but you are at a 6. Think about it though, where did you begin? Perhaps you started out at 2. If your relationship was at a 2 and now it is at a 6, that's a lot of progress you and your partner have made! This is why it is so important to keep your journal and to

continue to scale your progress along the way. If you don't, it is very easy to think of the small steps as flukes. Do not overlook the small steps as they are the building blocks for your ultimate goal. Relationships don't change overnight, as you know, and while the steps may be small, the overall progress is pretty big when you look at it over time. If you do not appreciate and recognize how far you have come, you will easily get discouraged. Relationships really do take work, infidelity or not, so note the small accomplishments along the way to stay positive.

4) **Reverting Back** – if things are not progressing well, you may want to look at your behaviors to assure that you have not started doing more of the same things that have not worked in the past. Ask yourself, when my spouse does a certain behavior that I do not like, what is my reaction to it and what is the behavior prior to it? Write these things down and note if they are the same behaviors you used to do when things were going poorly. If your progress during this healing process has improved, even just slightly, it means you are doing things right and moving in the right direction. Keep going. However, if you feel that progress has stopped or slowed dramatically, you may just not be doing what works so go back to Step 3 to readjust your techniques. It will make a difference.

The troubleshooting techniques are for you to use now that your relationship feels safe and trust continues to be established. However, setbacks are common and part of the recovery journey.

There may be instances when you do not feel safe or you feel that your partner is not making the needed changes. Chapter 9 addresses the most common problems.

It is my hope that you have no reason to read that chapter, but, in many cases, it is common that a spouse won't end an affair or won't commit to working on the marriage. If you are in such a situation, skip to Chapter 9 right now to address your particular issue. If not, keep reading on to keep the positive changes going.

Keeping it Going!

From this point on, you need to keep the communication going in your relationship and solve problems along the way. The two main tools you will use are: Maintenance Meetings and Conflict Resolution Meetings.

Before I begin telling you about these tools, you should first take stock of what is working in your relationship. What have you and your partner been doing to improve things? Get out your journal and ask yourself the following questions:

1. What have I been doing that has created positive changes in my relationship?

2. What has my partner been doing that has created positive changes in our relationship?

3. What do I need to continue to do in order for positive changes to keep going in our relationship?

4. What does my partner need to keep doing in order for positive changes to continue in our relationship?

Ask yourself these questions and encourage your partner to answer them with you. At this point, you should be working pretty well as a team. Just remember that you cannot expect things to continue to go well if you regress into old behaviors. You need to see how you and your partner came to such a good point in your relationship so that you can keep moving in a positive direction.

Remember those meetings that you have been having to talk about the affair and any needs that you have? It is time to change these meetings up for different purposes – to keep the positive changes going. Below, you will read about these weekly/biweekly meetings that you and your partner should set up in order for your progress to continue in a positive direction. Don't ignore them because these will be the primary tools to help you build a strong partnership that is infidelity-proof.

Maintenance Meetings

The best way that you and your partner can continue to grow in your relationship is to communicate in a positive way. These Maintenance Meetings are your tools for ongoing success in your long term relationship. This amazingly humble technique will help you for years on end. A Maintenance Meeting will allow you to compose a sacred place where you and your partner have the opportunity to talk about where you are in your relationship without any feedback or interruptions from the other.

What this meeting structure also allows you to do is: 1) engage with a partner that is attentively listening to what you are saying without trying to reply while you are speaking, and 2) truly hear your partner and what your partner thinks about your relationship.

Here is how it works:

1) You and your partner should arrange a slot of time for your maintenance session for at least 20 minutes and up to an hour. It really depends on what you can do in terms of your responsibilities and lifestyle, but I would not recommend any shorter than 20 minutes.

2) During your allotted time, let's call it 20 minutes for simplicity's sake, you and your partner will have an even distribution of time to speak. In this case, you and your partner will each have 10 minutes.

3) For your Maintenance Meeting, arrange a private and quiet place without any disruptions, that means telephones, televisions, and, of course, children. If you have children, make sure that they are supervised by another adult if appropriate or perhaps they are in school or day care at this time.

4) During the meeting, you should consume no alcohol or drugs nor should you be snacking or eating. Basically, no distractions whatsoever and no multitasking, no matter how small it may seem.

5) When you first begin your meeting, it does not matter who starts speaking. You can flip a coin or decide between the two of you. After the first session, the first speaker will always be the one who listened first during the previous meeting.

6) If you are the speaker, you will have 10 minutes to talk about your relationship and what you desire or need. You can include events of the day or past situations or anything as long as it involves your relationship. The only thing that you can't talk about is something you are angry over. This will be saved for the Conflict Resolution Meeting, described after this section. Be sure that you follow these rules because this Maintenance Meeting is a tool for you and your partner to dramatically help your positive progress in terms of trust and intimacy. It needs to be used correctly so, when in doubt, avoid topics of anger.

7) As the speaker, you need to avoid blaming your partner for anything, and you should only use "I" statements. Avoid "you" statements. So instead of saying, "You don't appreciate my dropping by at work to see you for lunch," say, "I feel sad because I feel like dropping over by your work isn't something you like." You can also discuss positive feelings that you have about your relationship. For instance, you might want to say, "I loved that you sent me flowers for my birthday yesterday."

8) You have 10 minutes to say anything you want in those parameters outlined above. If you run out of things to say before your 10 minutes is up, you and your partner should just sit and look at each other in silence. Continue to make eye contact. I find that in the silent moments, new topics arise that you may not have thought of before so honor this silence if you are left with nothing left to say.

9) Your partner will be listening during your speaking time, and he or she should listen fully without thinking of any responses. In fact, the listener will have no chance to respond to anything that the speaker is discussing so thinking about responses is really fruitless for this exercise. The only instance when the listener can respond is if he or she needs the speaker to repeat something that wasn't heard.

10) After your time is over as the speaker, you and your partner will switch roles. You will become the listener and your partner will become the speaker. As the second speaker, your partner will not respond to anything that you said in this session. If your partner has a response, that response needs to be saved for the next Maintenance Meeting. Your partner, at this point, should only discuss his or her wants and needs about the relationship, feelings about the past, and anything that comes up about the relationship, except for anything that is an anger issue.

11) Once you and your partner have had your turns, each 10 minutes for a 20 minutes session, the maintenance meeting is over. To close the meeting, hug or kiss one another. Whatever feels comfortable to bring the meeting to a close should be done at the end.

In the beginning, you may find that the meeting is awkward and difficult to do. This is normal as it will take practice to work through this exercise. The more that you do it, the better you will both be at it. It may feel artificial at first, but do not be discouraged or give up on the exercise.

Continue, and these meetings will do your relationship a wealth of good for years on end. You and your partner should commit to at least two Maintenance Meetings a week if you can. At the minimum, you can do one meeting a week, but I really suggest that you do two weekly for at least the first month.

As you continue the Maintenance Meetings, you will realize a lot about the way that the two of you communicate in addition to getting feedback about one another's feelings and wants and needs. You will also have a lot of realizations about the way that you listen to your partner, and this will be very helpful for you when the two of you are communicating day to day.

These maintenance meetings are excellent for communication, but they are also really excellent for getting closer to one another. Because they are scheduled regularly, you are forced to talk about your relationship and troubleshoot before problems get bigger. Remember, a big reason for the infidelity is because you and your partner had grown apart. You want to avoid this in the future as you build trust and intimacy year to year.

As the speaker, you will increase your emotional awareness and your emotional honesty about your relationship, and as the listener, you will learn how to listen deeply without forming responses back. This is quite powerful, and most couples struggle with this kind of communication. The more Maintenance Meetings you do, the better you will feel about your relationship and the deeper your friendship will become. These are so powerful so keep using them week to week, and do not feel discouraged about feeling awkward at first. Practicing will make your meetings more and more beneficial as you continue engaging with your spouse.

Conflict Resolution Meetings

Now let's discuss issues that anger you. When something your partner does angers you, take a step back and a timeout. In most cases, arguing in the heat of the moment is not productive. Tempers flare and emotions escalate in those instances, and not much progress is made. In most cases, the situation is exacerbated and becomes worse. You want to avoid this. This is not to say that you should not express your anger, but you want to resolve issues and express anger in a productive manner.

When your partner makes you angry, take a timeout. You and your partner should have an agreement about what do in heated situations. You or your partner can say, "We need to take a timeout and set up a Conflict Resolution Meeting." After you have stated that you need a timeout, you will leave your partner's presence to write about your feelings using the Peace Process (outlined next) in preparation of your Conflict Resolution Meeting.

Before you start writing, schedule a Conflict Resolution Meeting with your partner as soon as the both of you can make the time. Make sure that the time is free of distractions just as you have done for your Maintenance Meetings. If you and your partner are very busy, you can switch out a Maintenance Meeting for a Conflict Resolution Meeting. After all, life is busy and we need to make compromises and accommodations for life's responsibilities.

The Peace Process: A Written Exercise

After you and your partner have set up a time and day for your meeting, you need to start writing. This writing activity is called the Peace Process, and it is composed of five steps.

Each step requires you to write at least one sentence. In the following paragraphs, I provide you with sentence stems to get you started. Use the sentence stem that is appropriate for your situation. You don't have to use every sentence stem, and you can repeat the same sentence stem for a certain step if you like. You can use as many sentence stems as you like for each step. The only exception is the Anger Step. For the Anger Step, keep your sentences to a limit of four. This is done because the Anger Step needs to be expressed with limitations due to its inflammatory nature.

Provided below you have each step outlined along with various sentence stems. Start with the Anger Step and end with the Empathy Step. You should go in order as you write and so should you go in order when you discuss your Peace Process with your partner.

Think about your conflict and how you feel about it. Complete at least one sentence stem for each step. Go in order:

Anger Step:
I feel angry because…
I feel betrayed because…
I am resentful over…
I feel frustrated over…
It annoyed me when…
I was irritated because…
I am inpatient with…

Sadness Step:
It makes me sad when…
I feel grief when…
I am disappointed over…
I feel hurt because…
I feel despair over…

Fear Step:
I have fear over...
I feel anxious because...
I am worried about...
I am insecure over...
I am jealous because...

Ownership Step:
I feel guilty because...
I have some shame over...
I feel responsible for...
I am embarrassed about...

Empathy Step:
I understand that...
I appreciate that...
I am grateful for...
I have compassion for...
I admire that...
I love that...

After you have written out your Peace Process, bring that written process into your Conflict Resolution Meeting. You will read each statement to your partner starting with the Anger Step and ending with the Empathy Step. After you say each sentence, your partner should repeat your sentence to you verbatim or as close to verbatim as possible.

Once you and your partner have finished going through your Peace Process, your partner may be ready for a conflict resolution. You both may come up with a compromise or an agreement due to hearing your Peace Process. In another case, your partner may feel angry about something that you stated through your process, and in this case, your partner should take a timeout and do the exact same exercise about his or her anger issue that has arisen, starting with the Anger Step and ending with the Empathy Step.

After your partner has completed the Peace Process, you and your partner should start the exercise again, this time you will be the listener and your partner will be the speaker. Your partner will state each sentence, starting with the Anger Step, and you will repeat each sentence verbatim.

Here is an example of how this process might look:

Anger Step:
Speaker: I'm frustrated that you didn't ask me before you made plans with John and Daisy.
Listener: You're frustrated that I didn't ask you before I made plans with John and Daisy.

Speaker: I also resent that you didn't first check with me at work because I will be working late.
Listener: repeats verbatim

Sadness Step:
Speaker: I'm hurt that it didn't occur to you that I might want to just spend the night with you.
Listener: repeats verbatim

Fear Step:
Speaker: I fear that you don't want to spend alone time with me like you used to.
Listener: repeats verbatim

Speaker: I'm insecure about the weight I gained, and I guess I don't think you find me attractive anymore.
Listener: repeats verbatim

Ownership Step:
Speaker: I take responsibility for working too much, and I know I don't clearly tell you that I will be working late.
Listener: repeats verbatim

Speaker: I feel guilty that I make work more of a priority, and I don't take initiative to schedule a date night with you like I used to.
Listener: repeats verbatim

Empathy Step:
Speaker: I really appreciate that you take so much initiative for scheduling a date night every week.
Listener: repeats verbatim

Speaker: I also feel compassion because I know that our friends can be pushy, and you have a hard time telling them no.
Listener: repeats verbatim

Speaker: I love that you are so thoughtful of our friends' feelings and that you don't put pressure on me to schedule date nights because I am so busy at work.
Listener: repeats verbatim

Not surprisingly, going through this process often resolves the anger in itself. By the time you get to the meeting, you often have come to an understanding about your responsibility in the process, but that is not always the case. On many occasions, it may be that your partner is responsible for the situation that you were angry about. In that case, you may think that taking the ownership step is pointless, but what this exercise forces you to do is make a choice to build an empathic bridge with your partner. You choose to be a team in your relationship and so, even in circumstances when you feel your partner has wronged you, you team up with your partner and share in the responsibility anyway. That is really powerful, and in itself, it is healing.

What this Peace Process enables you to do is express your feelings in the first three steps and become a team again in the last two steps. Most importantly, the Peace Process moves you past the need to be right. It helps you go beyond the problem together rather than letting it rule your relationship. It turns your relationship into a partnership rather than a feud. When you and your partner embrace your problems as a team, you can surpass almost anything.

If you are this far in the book and are continuing to work with your mate, you have surpassed some difficult and tumultuous roads. Do not let the small bumps get the best of you. Communicate clearly about how important you are to one another and continue to participate as a team. Everything good really is possible, and you and your partner are living proof. You've done the hard work, and you can expect better things to come.

Chapter 8:
What You Can Expect After Completing the 7 Step Plan

I want to congratulate you on coming so far and doing this incredibly difficult work since you may have felt like giving up on many occasions. If you are reading this chapter, I assume that you have worked through the 7 Step Plan and that you are continuing to keep your positive changes going. Here are some things you can expect after going through the program.

Behavioral Changes Equal Solutions

As you change your behaviors, solutions are imminent. It is important to remember that blaming is not productive for positive progress and that if you want results, you need to put ego aside. Think of relationships as interactions that are circular. It is true that one action causes another reaction, but in relationships, actions and reactions are actually cyclical.

In a linear fashion, it is easy to think, if Betty spends more time at home, Andrew will feel more secure. However, it is much more than that. Andrew feels insecure, but he also feels insecure because Betty does not spend as much time at home. He does not feel like he is a priority in her life. If he feels more like a priority, he might feel more secure.

You see, it is not about an either or situation. It is both. In this kind of thinking, blame has no place because there is no beginning and no end. It's like the chicken and the egg problem – which one came first?

Was Andrew insecure before Betty spent less time at home? Perhaps, but the problems still goes round and round since one thing has an inevitable impact on another. When you think of behaviors in this way, it is easier to change starting with yourself. You have, of course, been doing these kinds of behavioral changes throughout the 7 Step Plan so you know a bit about this now. Just keep these points in mind when you start to feel resentful or want to place blame. Remember you are a team, and change can always start with one person.

Feelings Don't Have to Rule Behaviors

While feelings are always considerations, and you cannot control your feelings, you *can* control your behaviors. You can choose to put your resentments aside, even though you feel them, and act differently in order to generate different solutions. As you change your behaviors, your partner will react to those changes – just like a seesaw, as one side goes down, the other goes up. As you begin to see changes in your spouse, your feelings will change about your spouse as well. It is really powerful, and while it might be difficult to act differently than how you feel, it is possible, and it is, in many cases, more productive.

Your relationship will be better for it. Pay attention to the subtle changes when you behave in more productive ways. If something works, keep doing it. If you get responses that you don't like, change your pattern and observe.

Keep tweaking until you get the response you desire, and write about your changes and the responses that you receive in your journal so that you can know what you need to change and when you are making positive progress.

The Hurt You Feel Won't Change Right Away

Realize that you will have some bad days along the way and prepare for those days with your partner. On many days, you will feel resentful or angry. You might still feel betrayed or insecure. On those days, ask your spouse for reassurance. Work as a team together. As time goes by, you will have more good days, and trust will be reestablished. Intimacy between the two of you will be much stronger because of the team effort you put forth in healing from the infidelity.

Expect hurt feelings to come and expect bad days. That is normal, and you should not feel discouraged when you have a bad day. It is part of the healing journey. On those days, you can lean heavier on your partner to help you through the day. If you are feeling insecure, ask your partner to reassure you about his or her commitment to your relationship. If you are feeling angry about something, set up a Conflict Resolution Meeting. If you are feeling sad, discuss your feelings with your partner and work together as a team.

Take care of yourself. Sometimes, you may need time on your own, and your partner may not be able to help you through every bad day. Do not expect your partner to carry the entire load. Sometimes it is okay for you to take a break and practice self-care.

Your Relationship Can Be Saved After Infidelity

The most important point to remember in terms of expectations is that your relationship *can* be saved after infidelity.

If you and your partner do the work, you don't have to assume that your relationship is over. You and your partner can rebuild trust and intimacy. In fact, you and your partner can build an even stronger relationship than you had in the first place. Now that's something to look forward to! While it will not be instantaneous and while it won't always be easy, it is very possible to rebuild a crumbling partnership. I have seen it time after time working with couples. The commitment that you have with your partner will be stronger and closer as you learn and grow together through the healing process. You and your partner can do this.

Realizing When It's Time to Move On

In some cases, it may be best to move on from your relationship. Before you make this choice, read through Chapter 9, *Advanced Strategies*, to pinpoint your issue and what you can do to address it. It may be that a certain problem you thought was unsolvable can be solved. In some cases, the best decision might be to move on, but I have found that most couples that work the plan come out stronger together in the end. Be honest with yourself, but be realistic. Also, know your own limits.

Section 3: Addressing Unique Situations & Common Problems

Chapter 9: Advanced Strategies

"Progress is impossible without change, and those who cannot change their minds cannot change anything."

- George Bernard Shaw

As you take this healing journey, you might hit a few road bumps along the way. Every relationship is different and has its unique challenges. If you find that you and your partner are stuck due to an issue that has arisen, you will, most likely, find the answer in this chapter. If you don't find the answer or need additional help with your healing, there is a resource for you! Log on to www.infidelitysurvivalplan.com, and check out the other means of help.

When Your Partner Won't End the Affair

You might be in a situation where your partner refuses to end the affair. If this is the case, you might feel that there is no hope, but I want to assure you that there still is hope. Most affairs end within six months, and they do not often result in a marriage. If they do, they have a higher chance of divorce – about 60%. So you want to reconcile with your partner, it might be a matter of waiting the affair out.

While waiting may seem daunting, there are a few things that you can do during the waiting period to create more positive changes for you and your estranged spouse. Just know that you need to prepare yourself for a tough battle, and you will need to set your negative feelings aside many times in order to get through this time. The things you need to do will be difficult. It is so hard to recover from a betrayal all on your own, especially when your partner is not supportive or loving towards you. However, it is possible to still save your relationship even if your partner is unwilling to give up the affair partner.

If you are choosing to fight for your relationship, you need to promise yourself that you will no longer pursue your partner. What I mean is that you need to stop pushing your partner for change, pleading that your partner give up the affair; you need to stop pursuing your partner altogether. I realize, perhaps, that this might sound counterintuitive, but if you continue to chase your partner around, you will experience the seesaw effect of your actions. Your partner will run away from you because of your chasing, and the affair partner will become a much more attractive option.

Stopping to pursue your partner means that you have to discourage yourself from calling your partner, begging your partner to reconsider, and pointing out all the good that your partner is missing out on in your relationship. You have to stop following your partner around, whether that is around the house or, if your partner has moved out, do not follow your partner in your car. You cannot write letters, and you cannot send emails. Also, stop saying, "I love you."

While this might be very difficult for you, be aware that your estranged partner does not hear "I love you" when you say it. Your partner hears, "Please reconsider," and your "I love you" sounds just like another chasing technique. Do not chase at all.

Next, you need to put energy towards yourself and your interests. In this stage of your relationship, you will be feeling down and insecure. This is understandable. You will cry a lot, and you will probably lose interest in a lot of things. However, if you continue to nurse these feelings, it will be even more difficult to be patient and wait your partner's affair out. Take care of yourself.

Ask yourself what you're interested in. Ask yourself how you can make yourself feel better, even for a little while. What is it about you that attracted your partner to you in the first place? You might have been very motivated or very cheerful. You might have been very optimistic or energetic. I realize that you're probably not feeling any of those things right now because this is such an awful time for you. However, fight against those feelings. You will have bad days and even worse days, but you need to start to do something that you enjoy. Perhaps you are a foodie and you love trying new restaurants. Go out there on your own and find the restaurants you always wanted to try. You can start a hobby if you enjoy certain crafts or collecting items. If you are sporty, join a league or start jogging. Do something for yourself. Go to the spa once a week or start a community garden. The possibilities are really quite endless so do what will make you the happiest while you are in this difficult situation.

After you start doing some things for yourself, you will find that your disposition will change a bit. You will be taking care of yourself while simultaneously getting back those traits your partner loved about you.

The benefits are really twofold. After you do these things, sit back and wait. Your partner will probably start to show interest in you again.

It is not definite that your partner will come back to you even when you try these things. However, by doing the things that I outlined, you have a much better chance of success. It may still be that your partner shuts the door on your relationship and moves on. In that case, you will need to heal yourself even more so it just makes self-care even more important, no matter what the results.

More likely, your partner may become curious about the changes you're making in your life. Your partner might start showing more interest in you and wondering what you're up to in your life. He or she might even want to spend more time with you than before. All of this is possible, and I have seen it with individuals I have worked with. If this starts to happen, be respectful, and be loving to your partner, but do not be overambitious. If your he or she invites you somewhere, spend that time together, but if you made plans for yourself or with a friend, do not cancel those plans.

When you and your spouse are together, refrain from asking about your future together, and continue to be as positive as you can be. Under no circumstances should you say, "I love you" now. If your partner says, "I love you" then you can reciprocate, but leave it at that – just an "I love you too" will suffice for now. Do not chase. Do not start a conversation about your relationship.

Most importantly, keep physical intimacy boundaries. If your partner has not cut off the relationship with the affair partner, be kind and be loving, but do not be physically intimate. Under no circumstances should you spend the night or engage in any sexual activity with your partner at this point.

Continue to take care of yourself, and if your partner asks to reconcile, this is when you can arrange a meeting to discuss the things that you will and will not tolerate.

The most important thing you should not tolerate is continued contact with the affair partner. Assure there is a clean break, and ask that your partner make the contact with the affair partner in your presence. Your partner can call the affair partner on the phone while you are in the room and state, "I want to work things out in my relationship, and I can no longer continue contact with you." Reread Step 1 of the plan for more guidance about making clean breaks with the affair partner.

When Your Partner is Resistant

Your partner might have agreed to reconcile, but as you start the healing process, you may find that your partner is resistant. Perhaps your partner is unwilling to carry out some of the specific requests that you both outlined for proper healing. You can spot the resistance whenever you hear something like, "Yes, but..." Perhaps your partner is saying, "Yes, I want to work on the marriage, but this just seems like more work then we need to do."

Resistance is normal. After all, change is difficult, and this might just be part of your healing journey. If you or your partner are resistant, identify the resistance so that you can both address it.

Above all, do not wait on your partner to initiate change just because you feel that you are in the right. You might be, but remember that behaviors create changes, not feelings, and certainly not blame. Sometimes people are scared of changes. There are many reasons for resistance. Either way, you can start initiating behavioral changes in order to get the seesaw moving in a more productive manner.

You can try some of the behavioral changes in Step 3 or you can hold a Conflict Resolution Meeting (outlined in Step 7). Depending on how the resistance started, you can identify the appropriate plan.

A Sexually Addicted Partner

You may be concerned that your partner has a sexual addiction, and this is a significant concern. It may be that your partner is spending hours of time on the Internet cruising craigslist or chat rooms to find partners. It could be a pornography addiction. It could be prostitutes, strippers, or affair partners. Whatever it is, if it is excessive and out of control, you might be dealing with the consequences of your partner's sexual addiction. If you fear that this might be the case, here is a list of reading resources depending on your concerns and circumstances:

Out of the Shadows: Understanding Sexual Addiction by Patrick Carnes

Healing the Wounds of Sexual Addiction by Mark Laaser

In the Shadows of the Net: Breaking Free of Compulsive Online Sexual Behavior by Patrick Carnes & David Delmonico

Losing the Bond with God: Sexual Addiction and Evangelical Men by Kailla Edger

Cruise Control: Understanding Sexual Addiction in Gay Men by Robert Weiss & Patrick Carnes

Mending a Shattered Heart: A Guide for Partners of Sex Addicts by Stefanie Carnes

Breaking the Cycle: Free Yourself from Sexual Addiction, Porn Obsession, and Shame by George Collins & Andrew Adleman

You can also contact a therapist who specializes in sexual addiction. The Society of Advancement of Sexual Health (SASH – www.sash.net) is a great resource, and you can find a list of many therapists who specialize in working with sexual addiction issues on their website. If your partner is willing to see a specialized therapist, I suggest you utilize therapy as part of your healing process.

If your partner is not willing to attend therapy, reread the above strategies for addressing resistance. Also, if your partner is not willing to give up any of his or her behaviors, reread the first section of this chapter (on resistance to giving up affair partners) to help you with some personal strategies.

If your partner is obsessed with or addicted to any sexual behavior, your partner will not make the decision to change unless some losses are experienced. Your partner may still need to realize that the sexual addiction is a serious problem. If this is the case, you will need to deliver an ultimatum.

Whether it is delivered in a letter, in an email, or face-to-face, let your partner know that addressing the sexual addiction needs to be part of the healing steps or you cannot continue with the relationship. Sexual addiction is not a clear-cut behavior, so you both might have your doubts about whether it is an issue.

If you think you can progress without therapy, go through this 7 Step Plan, and see how it works for you. Be sure that you set appropriate boundaries for your partner. If your partner has excessively gone online to cruise Internet sites for partners, you will need to set up the computer in a public place and set limits on its use.

A specialized therapist can guide you through this procedure and so can many of the books I mentioned previously.

How to Handle Holidays and Special Events

Family life is full of celebrations and rituals such as birthdays, weddings, and graduations. Having to pretend that you are content in your relationship while you are both going through the healing stages of infidelity can be very difficult. Putting on a façade that you are a committed couple when the commitment is very unstable is difficult and can have a negative impact on your healing. However, you cannot give up your families and friends, and special occasions will probably occur during the time you and your partner are flailing. When you and your partner are invited to an event or have to host a celebration for family or friends, you can plan together in a concrete way. Talk to each other about what you will expect from the day and what kinds of challenges you will need to overcome.

Talk about where you are in your relationship in terms of time. It is often the case that you will compare your relationship this year to last year. For instance, "Last Christmas, we were so happy, and this holiday season is so awful. I feel like everything is falling apart!" You may feel resentful because the infidelity has "destroyed" your celebration. This is understandable. You will need to talk about these feelings, and I suggest using a Conflict Resolution Meeting to talk through any feelings of anger. This way, you and your partner can arrive at a compromise about what you both need to do while you both express your feelings about the upcoming event.

You and your partner may need to limit the guest list or use a code word when one of you needs a timeout. You may talk about certain triggers that will come up, and how you will handle those triggers. Think about the potential challenges, talk about your feelings using that Peace Process, and work together towards a concrete plan for the upcoming event.

How to Handle Relapses and Setbacks

Setbacks are part of the healing process so it is important to be realistic about those. At the same time, setbacks are different than relapses. A setback is a small slip that requires only a quick recovery while a relapse is a regression to a prior state of destructiveness. Relapses can happen when you and your partner get too discouraged, too fearful, or too tired. Basically, when you and your partner are not communicating well for some time and, therefore, not interacting well, a relapse is something to be concerned about.

This is why it is so important to continue with your Maintenance Meetings. Just having these meetings will help you avoid relapses in the future. If a relapse does occur, give yourself a timeout, and step back. This will allow both of you to calm down first. After this, ask yourself what has happened and what you can do differently in the future.

You and your partner can discuss setbacks in a Conflict Resolution Meeting using the Peace Process as a tool. Don't forget your agreement for taking a timeout when it is needed. It is my hope that a relapse does not occur, and I don't foresee a relapse happening if you continue having Maintenance Meetings.

However, things do happen in life. Remember that you and your partner are a team, and you should proceed as such. Avoid blame in such a situation. Remember to be as respectful as you can, and be kind.

If you and your partner are consistently communicating in a productive manner, relapses are minimal if not completely absent. If you and your partner have a setback, use the Conflict Resolution Meeting to help you process your feelings and discuss responsibilities on each side. After this, you and your partner can discuss a plan to get you both back on track. Setbacks are inevitable so expect them. If you are not feeling angry, but you fear that a setback might be imminent, you can discuss your concern in your next Maintenance Meeting – whatever you feel is appropriate and depending on how you feel in terms of anger.

Self-Care

Above all, you and your partner both need to take care of yourselves. It is important for you to take care of yourself because repairing your relationship and healing from betrayal is difficult and emotionally draining. Living with continuous stress is destructive both physically and emotionally. Do something you love. Start a hobby, join a group, begin a movement, etc.

Take care of yourself physically. Being active is one of the best things you can do for yourself to help elevate your mood and keep yourself physically and emotionally well. Pay attention to your diet. Eat well, and drink lots of fluids. Avoid alcohol and drugs as appropriate.

Above all, find laughter in your life. Laughter is one of the best ways to enhance your mood and immune system. Watch comedies together; read silly books; ride a roller coaster, whatever makes you laugh and brings you joy.

Meditation and yoga are also very helpful for stress reduction and building a more positive life. Meditation has been scientifically proven to help people decrease stress and increase focus. You need those things at this time! If you are interested in yoga, avoid hot yoga or anything too vigorous for stress reduction purposes. However, if you truly enjoy those types of yoga practices, do not omit them out of your life.

Reintroducing Physical Intimacy

Throughout this journey, it might be difficult to start being physically intimate again with one another. You and your partner may feel awkward and uncomfortable incorporating sexuality back into your relationship.

It can be a huge stressor at first so give yourself and your spouse some time away from it. Take it off the menu. Make an agreement that you and your partner will set sexual intimacy aside for the first 3 months as you begin to work through the 7 Step Plan together. This takes the pressure off of both of you.

As you and your partner meet together to discuss your relationship, incorporate discussions about your sex life and how you feel about physical intimacy at that point. When you and your partner both agree that you feel comfortable enough to reintroduce physical intimacy back into your relationship, you can proceed from there. Remember that you can take it slowly.

You can begin with hugging, kissing, heavy patting, etc. instead of jumping right into intercourse. If you both feel ready before the initial 3 months have passed, you can start reintroducing sexual intimacy earlier. Just be sure you are both emotionally ready.

When Medication is Considered

If you feel that you need more support than what you can do on your own or what you can get from your partner, you may want to consider talking to a licensed mental health professional. If you or your partner are having a difficult time functioning in your daily lives or if either of you are homicidal or suicidal, do not hesitate to call an expert to help you through. You may need some antidepressant or anti-anxiety medications to help you cope. In some cases, the medication is temporary to get you over the hump.
It will be up to you and your provider to come up with an appropriate plan. Do what is right for you and your partner, and do not discredit the possibility of needing medication if you are unable to manage on your own. With that said, I hope that I have given you many suggestions to help you with your emotional well-being through self-care practices.

Chapter 10: Avoiding Infidelity in the Future

The most important task for avoiding infidelity in the future of your relationship is to maintain good boundaries in friendships. It is very easy to cross the line with a friend, and before you know it, you could end up in dangerous intimate territory. Also, avoiding problems within your marriage also causes more distance and can be a breeding ground for infidelity so stay connected and updated with one another.

Below, I have outlined some of the most important things to remember to protect your future relationship from infidelity, whether you are protecting the current relationship you have healed through or if you are moving on to a new venture.

1) Maintain good boundaries with friends and your partner. Be sure that you are open with your partner, and be private (as appropriate) with friends. You can test your current friendships by asking yourself the question, "If my partner heard and saw everything that I talked about and did with my friend, would my partner have any problems with it?" If you would have no problem with your partner seeing or hearing how you engaged and talked with a friend, you are in a safe zone. Continue to ask yourself this question with all your friendships, and you will be on the right track in keeping appropriate boundaries.

2) Be aware that the workplace is one of the biggest danger zones for affairs. If you find yourself spending more and more time with one certain co-worker during lunches and coffee breaks, ask yourself about your boundaries. You may need to scale back the time you spend with one another or turn the one-on-one meetings into group meetings. Invite a few other co-workers along for lunch.

3) Be sure that you are not too supportive of a friend who is confiding in you about his or her failing relationship. Often times, we find somebody attractive with whom we bond because of a relationship that is going south; boundaries can start to blur, and the closeness of a friendship might turn into something else. If your friend or coworker talks to you excessively about a failing relationship, redirect the conversation or let your friend know that, perhaps, he or she should speak with his or her partner instead.

4) If you are having any issues with your relationship, discuss it with your spouse. If you feel that you need to talk to somebody else about your relationship, make sure that the person you speak to is supportive of your relationship. Do not get into divisive discussions with other people about your partner.

5) Avoid old boyfriends and girlfriends. If you have a former lover that you see at a class reunion or who "friends" you on Facebook, for instance, invite your partner to come along to the event or avoid "friending" the old flame on any social media sites. If you want to keep your relationship safe from the risk of infidelity, avoid old flames altogether.

6) Be careful online with the acquaintances you have on the Internet. Make sure that your partner is aware of all of your online friendships, and be open with your email, Facebook, and any other Internet tools you are using to engage with friends. Never exchange any sexual fantasies or any information of a sexual nature online.

7) Make sure that your friends and family are all supportive of your relationship. Surround yourself with people who are happy in their relationships and who do not believe in stepping out with another partner.

Now that you have all of the tools to heal from the infidelity and strategies to avoid infidelity in the future, let me walk you through some steps to prevent sabotaging all the progress you have already made. In the following chapter, I outline four of the most common sabotaging thoughts and behaviors you might encounter during the 7 Step Plan so read on.

Chapter 11: Preventing Sabotage

You have been asked to make a lot of behavioral changes with your partner as well as do some things that may feel awkward. I want you to know that I have worked with many couples and have developed this plan because it works. At times, however, you might feel discouraged or question certain techniques so I have outlined a few common concerns. Be honest about your thoughts and how you may be sabotaging your progress as you read through so that you can address thoughts and behaviors appropriately.

This is Manipulative

You might be thinking that changing your behaviors in spite of how you feel is a manipulation. Well, it is, in all respects. However, this is not a bad thing. Manipulation is essential in the change process. You can manipulate negatively or positively. In fact, we manipulate day to day as we live our lives. I do A to get B. If you are not feeling well because you and your partner got into a fight, but you have to be upbeat for a work meeting, you change your attitude in order to get the job done. Otherwise, you know that you would have more problems on your hands. We adjust our behaviors all the time in order to get better results and make our lives work for us.

Working on your relationship is no different. It may feel like it is unnatural to behave in different ways than how you are feeling, but what good is it to act on your feelings if those behaviors are destroying your relationship?

What I am teaching you is that you do not have to be a slave to your feelings. You can react in more positive ways despite how you feel so that you can get more positive outcomes. Relationships take work, but we often don't realize that we need to do something different until a crisis hits. Infidelity is often the crisis that makes us step back and think about what we need to do to turn things around in our relationships. Changing your behaviors to better suit your relationship is manipulative, and it is the best manipulation possible – a manipulation that edifies rather than a manipulation that destroys. It is for the good of you and your partner's future, and while you are adjusting your behaviors, your partner will be adjusting behaviors as well. This is a good thing!

Emotional Ambushes

Applying many of the skills in this book can be difficult due to how you feel about your partner at times. The state of your relationship can make you want to say and do things that will derail you from your ultimate goal. No matter how determined you are, at some point, your emotions might get the better of you. Expect this to happen. When you are feeling emotionally overwhelmed or negative feelings are taking over your determination, re-read Step 5 to help you overcome negative thoughts and feelings.

This journey is not easy, by any means, and you will have a lot of ups and downs. Expecting that your emotions might get the better of you from time to time, you should be armed with solutions when negativity strikes. As you move through the healing process and you take note of your small successes with your partner, it will become easier for you to continue on.

Note the positive changes that are occurring in your journal, and read over them when negative emotions strike. By developing a focus on past positive achievements, you will be able to stay on track. Your relationship will not be turned around instantaneously and so hard work and determination will be needed.

At this point, you have all the tools necessary to take this journey and successfully heal form the trauma of infidelity so highlight the important parts that strike you in this book so that you can utilize the tools you need most when things get difficult. Lastly, remember that learning how to repair your relationship will take patience as well as time and practice.

Shoulds

By all means, avoid the shoulds! "My marriage should be easy." "This process shouldn't be so hard." "Relationships should work well if you are with the right person." Nonsense. None of those statements are correct, but many people fail because they focus on such unrealistic expectations. A long-term relationship takes a lot of work, and there is no "should" for any one individual relationship. Every relationship is different, and your relationship will be what you make it. It *shouldn't* be one way or another.

As you work with your partner, your relationship will become what you want it to be. Getting stuck in the idea of "should" is one of the most destructive mind frames many couples get into. When you find yourself using that word, think about your statement, and throw it out the window. *You* have the power to change your relationship. So here's the only should statement that is important – your relationship *should* be what you make it.

Comparing Your Relationship

When your relationship is not going well, it is easy to compare your relationship to a potential new one. You might think, "If I were with someone else, I wouldn't have to put up with this difficulty." While that may be true, other difficulties would inevitably arise in new relationships. Don't kid yourself. No relationship is perfect, and every relationship passes through a storming stage. We bring our expectations of what we think our and our partner's role should be into every new partnership. Our partners do this too so there is always an adjustment period in every relationship. You will face difficulty in every relationship you have, and what you once thought was a benefit to your new partner's personality will become an annoyance.

If it's possible, the best way to having a happy relationship is working through the problems and issues you have in your current one. In some cases, it may be that you need to leave your relationship, and this will be something you will have to come to terms with. However, I find that in most long-term relationships, problems are resolvable. It's just that most couples do not have the proper tools for long-term intimacy, and *that* is why divorce happens 50% of the time. I guess that might be obvious to you at this point.

If you have the proper tools to work together, then you can succeed in your relationship. No new relationship is a magic bullet, and if you are comparing your problematic relationship to someone else's relationship that might be in the honeymoon stage, you will always be at a loss. Just like the affair partner in your spouse's relationship was a honeymoon relationship, so is your comparison to someone else's bliss or your idea of what an ideal relationship might be. Be realistic and keep going if you feel your relationship is worth the fight.

On that note, if you are being abused or if your partner refuses to work with you on your relationship despite all of your behavioral changes and tools that you have used from this book, it might be time to move on. No one deserves to be abused, physically or emotionally, and if you are in such a situation, leave the relationship. In the end, it takes two individuals to make a long-term partnership successful so if your partner will not bend and is not willing to work with you, you are better off pressing forward with someone who deserves your energy.

Now that you have read about some of the most common sabotages for completing the program with success, ask yourself the following questions about each sabotage:

1. Did you make this mistake?

2. If so, what was the most painful part of making this mistake for you personally?

3. As someone dedicated to success, write down what you learned from this mistake.

4. What are three ideas you plan to implement to make sure that you don't make this mistake again?

Write the answers to these questions in your journal when appropriate. Find a strategy to help you avoid pitfalls, and if you have identified any of your own pitfalls that were not mentioned in this book, jot them down in your journal as well. Remember that you are worth the fight, and since you are reading this book, it is safe to assume that you are willing to work towards a positive long-term relationship. You deserve the same in return. I wish the best for you and your partner!

Chapter 12: Conclusion

You have come a long way, and I sincerely hope that you have found the 7 Step Infidelity Survival Plan helpful in healing from infidelity and making your relationship stronger than it ever was. I want you to know, again, that I have helped many couples through this process, and if they can do it, so can you. Because many individuals cannot afford therapy or might be challenged with time or money, this 7 Step Plan is constructed for you to be able to do it yourself, of course with your partner along! I hope that you know that many people just like you have succeeded with this program, and when mending the relationship seems impossible, they still gave it a try and were surprised at how great their relationship turned out. Wonderful things can happen for you too. In this final chapter, I have included a few testimonials from some of the people I have helped through the years. The names and identifying details have been changed to protect anonymity, but these are stories that are true and from people that have worked just as hard as you are preparing yourself to work. I hope that you find their stories inspiring.

Magda

I can remember when I first started working on this program, and I thought that my relationship was never going to revive. You told me that if I have even just a hint of desire to work towards repairing my relationship that I should give it a try.

Reluctantly, I decided to listen to your guidance. I can still remember how helpless I felt and how hurt I was. My husband had a long affair with a woman, and I never thought that I could love him again. I remember just wanting to stay for the kids, and while I thought that wasn't the best reason, it was my only motive. I can't even tell you how grateful I am that I made this decision. We had many ups and downs, and I wanted to give up a few times – many times! We worked through it, and our relationship is the strongest that it's ever been. We are still doing the Maintenance Meetings once a week, and I would have to say that this one tool has been our primary saving grace. We used to just yell at each other, and we had no idea how to communicate. Now we actually work through issues, and we tackle new ones. I love my husband so much, and it sounds crazy, but I'm almost grateful for the affair! If I wouldn't have had to go through this absolutely torturous time, it would never be this good now. Thank you for your help. I want to tell everybody that this works!

Eric

Jane and I are doing really well. I never knew how much better we could get. It's astounding to me that only last year we were on the verge of divorce. I can't believe how well this program has worked. Jane calls me from work every day on her lunch break just to tell me that she loves me, and it just never gets old. I hope you know how grateful we are that we found your book and your website and were able to work the program together. I don't think we could have done it without your tools.

I can't even believe that Jane had an affair. I'm just not married to the same woman anymore. Jane is happy, loving, and I genuinely feel secure in our relationship. It's just amazing. Thank you again for helping our marriage.

Joyce

I worked this program for just three months, and I still can't believe how quickly it worked. When My husband would not give up his mistress, and he was ready to move out. I was beside myself, but I knew that I wanted to save my marriage. I have to tell you that I wasn't very hopeful. As a last resort, I tried your program and used the techniques you taught me for working on myself even though my husband wanted out. Only after one month, he was curious about me again, and by two months, we were back together! I couldn't believe how quickly he turned around, and I know that I would never be where I am today with him if it wasn't for your program. Thank you so much for saving our relationship. We are still working through so many things, and we are still building trust in our relationship, but I know that it will just keep getting better.

In Closing

Now that you have read some stories from real couples, I hope you are inspired. It is my sincerest hope that the program will be just as successful for you just as it has been for the couples I have worked with. I have laid out my best tools and techniques, and I have seen the successes with clients.

I know that this plan can also work for you. I want to congratulate you on taking the first step towards a better future. It will get better!

References Used In Creating The 7 Step Infidelity Survival Plan

Askham, J. (1984). *Identity and stability in marriage.* Cambridge, MA: Cambridge University Press.

Barash, D. P. & Lipton, J. E. (2002). *The myth of monogamy: Fidelity and infidelity in animals and people.* Chicago, IL: Holt Paperbacks.

Buss, D. (2000). *The dangerous passion: Why jealousy is as necessary as love and sex.* New York: Free Press.

Davis, M. W. (2001). *The divorce remedy.* New York: Simon & Schuster. [You Must Guide the Way]

Davis, M. W. (1992). *Divorce busting.* New York: Simon & Schuster. [You Must Guide the Way]

De Angelis, B. (1991). *How to make love all the time: Make love last a lifetime.* New York: Random House Publishing Group. [Peace Process]

Glass, S. P. (2004). *Not "just friends": Rebuilding trust and recovering your sanity after infidelity.* New York: Free Press. [Managing Obsessions & Flashbacks]

Heatherington, E. M. & Kelly, J. (2002). *For better or worse: Divorce reconsidered.* New York: Norton.

Hindy, C. G., Schwarz, J. C., & Brodsky, A. (1989). *If this is love, why do I feel so insecure?* New York: Fawcett Books.

Hoobyar, T. & Dotz, T. (2013). *NLP: The essential guide to neuro-linguistic programming.* New York: Harper Collins. [Creating Anchors]

Kantor, D. (1999). *My lover, myself: Self-discovery through relationship.* New York: Riverhead Books.

Ortman, D. C. (2009). *Transcending post-infidelity stress disorder (PISD): The six stages of healing.* Berkeley, CA: Celestial Arts.

Taylor, M. & McGee, S. (2000). *The new couple: Why the old rules don't work and what does.* San Francisco, CA: Harper & Collins. [Maintenance Meeting]

Waite, L. J. & Gallagher, M. (2000). *The case for marriage: Why married people are happier, healthier, and better off financially.* New York: Doubleday.

*All of these resources have contributed to creating *Infidelity Survival Plan*. I have added specific interventions borrowed for some of these resources in an effort to give credit to the authors who created the interventions originally, and I recommend the books highly for further reading. In addition to pulling on my own clinical expertise, the above authors and experts have considerably contributed to my work. I thank you all, dear authors, for guiding my way.

- Dr. Kat Peoples

Reading this book is just the first step, and I have many more resources for your success as well as support. If you have any questions or are interested in further help, you can get more resources at **www.infidelitysurvivalplan.com**

- Dr. Kat Peoples

Made in the USA
Las Vegas, NV
29 March 2023

69839114R00090